Pilgrimage to Discipleship

A Guide to the Spiritual Exercises of Ignatius Loyola

Julius M. Rogina

Illustrations
Joyce Rossi

PILGRIMAGE TO DISCIPLESHIP

A Guide to the Spiritual Exercises of Ignatius Loyola

Library of Congress Control Number: 2019913888
ISBN-13: Paperback: 978-1-64398-996-9

Printed in the United States of America

LitFire LLC
1-800-511-9787
www.litfirepublishing.com
order@litfirepublishing.com

DEDICATION

This guide to the Spiritual Exercises of Ignatius Loyola is dedicated to the People of God of the Episcopal Diocese of Nevada.

Through the many years of facilitating the fourteen weeks of the Spiritual Exercises of Ignatius Loyola, I had printed the pages of this guide to serve as handouts to participants from our parishes from the northern part of the Diocese or what is known to us in the Diocese of Nevada as the Northwest District. This book is now the culmination of the input of many participants.

I am grateful to many who have supported this ministry, directly or indirectly, especially

The Rt. Rev. Dan Edwards, Retired Bishop of Episcopal Diocese of Nevada

and

The Very Rev. Dr. William L. Stomski, Dean and Rector of Trinity Episcopal Cathedral

I am grateful to Ms. Joyce Rossi who generously produced the illustrations for this project. When I asked her to consider making illustrations, she gave it some thought and surprised me with her gift of illustrations that you are privileged to see. She makes the following comment about the process of creating the illustrations:

> I was asked if I might want to do some illustrations for this book. The idea of using my craft in response to the Exercises was truly exciting. Mixing creativity with spirituality: what a unique recipe for joy. I used watercolor because of the symbolic meanings of water throughout the Bible. From the Genesis flood to the blood and water that flowed from our Savior's side, water is rich in meaning. The illustrations came from my own life experiences. But I hope they will open the door for your own creative interpretations as you encounter Jesus in your own journey through the Exercises of St. Ignatius.

There are many others who assisted this guide to come to birth: Debbie Zalmana, who helped with formatting and publishing; Maggie Wirtanen and Jeanne Hansen, who edited the text to make it more readable and who assisted with many helpful recommendations making the text appealing to a contemporary reader.

All for the Greater Glory of God!

Julius M. Rogina

Priest, Episcopal Diocese of Nevada and
Clinical Psychologist in Private Practice

CONTENTS

ABBREVIATIONS

AMDG	*Ad Majorem Dei Gloriam,* To the greater Glory of God
BCP	The Book of Common Prayers
Hymnal	The Hymnal 1982, Service Music
NRSV	The Holy Bible. (1989) Old and New Testaments with Apocrypha/ Deuterocanonical Books. Nashville: Thomas Nelson Publisher
SE	Puhl, L. J. (1951). The Spiritual Exercises of St. Ignatius. Chicago: Loyola University Press
S.J.	Indicates that the person is a member of the Society of Jesus

•

Permissions to print granted by the following authors:
Archbishop Rowan Williams, the story of Lulu, p. 11
Joyce M. Rossi, picture designs for movements of the Exercises, p. 13,18,31,51,63, and 73
Bishop Dan Edwards, reflections on Baptism, p. 34
John Ries, John Ries Photography, personal photo, p. 106

PREFACE

I trust you to be a spiritually curious person who is looking for some new ways of understanding and experiencing what spiritual pilgrimage is. Traditionally, spiritual pilgrimage is understood as a journey or a search into the understanding of one's own life and living. This book, or perhaps better termed a guidebook, invites you to embark on the pilgrimage toward increased spiritual health and resilience through a lens of one of the giants of Christian Spirituality by name Ignatius Loyola.

This is not a book like a novel or a treatise of some kind, be that a scientific inquiry or a philosophical expose. It is not a psychology book where you would learn about human motivation theories or human consciousness. It is a book that invites you to a deeper personal relationship with Jesus of history and the Christ of Christian worship. It is a book that will guide you to come to grips with the profound questions of human existence. It will challenge you to a personal relationship with the God that Jesus calls "Father." Strictly speaking, this book, this guide invites the one who enters the dynamics of the Spiritual Exercises into a personal relationship with the Holy One that some people call God and others Mystery and yet others the Ground of Being or an Ultimate Horizon of our desires.

The need to be shaken from spiritual lethargy is essential for making yourself spiritually awakened in your life and embarking on this kind of a pilgrimage. Engaging in the Spiritual Exercises of Ignatius Loyola could become the most important spiritual awakening in your life.

By now you have mastered many skills needed for a good life. You know how to ride a bicycle or drive a car, read, write and do math. You may have raised kids, developed niche skills for a career, and built a healthy family life. All these skills help make you successful in the world, but being spiritually awakened, however, requires a much different skill set. As we gradually awaken spiritually, we are often led to consider a new kind of lifestyle. Frequently, this new awareness can be awkward if not frightening. Some people stop right there. They pull back to what is familiar. Others make the necessary changes however small. They start organizing a different type of life that is based on spiritual values of kindness and loving justice with mercy—full of meaningful possibilities.

There is no need to be afraid. Ignatius says that God deals with each one of us in a unique and gentle way, as a caring teacher and life-giving guide (SE #1-21). As we read in the Gospel of John, we find out that God desires life for each one of us. "I have come in order that you might have life—life in all its fullness (John 10:10). The life God desires for us is uniquely ours, tailored to our specifications.

There are many notable paths to take to start the life of spiritual awakenings, to build our thirst as well as to satisfy our curiosity. What I present in this book, however, is a

Christian spiritual path that is based on Ignatian practice—just one of many that are found within the Christian spiritual traditions.

Ignatian Spiritual Exercises intend to open us up to new dimensions in our lives and invite us to walk on the path of life with a reinvigorated spiritual resilience that is uniquely Christian. We will soon discover that Spiritual Exercises can lead to a way of life that we can design together. Ignatius will introduce the concepts like discernment and election which mean to organize our living in such a way that "is totally in alignment" with our deepest desire to be honestly and authentically ourselves before the Holy One, the Ultimate reality of our life and living.

We will be introduced to a rhythm of prayer based on our awareness of God's presence in our lives and our awareness of the world around us. We will also learn how to pay more attention to our interior lives so that we can better discern our life's direction while remaining focused on values that embody the Gospels for the service of all God's People and all of God's creation.

In order to engage in the Spiritual Exercises of Ignatius Loyola, our awareness of the divine presence in the world, the sacred mystery about God, is necessary. Ignatius suggests that God actively works in the universe, the world around us, and within. In fact, Ignatius believes that God labors in everything for our good (SE #236).

Throughout the Exercises Ignatius continually presupposes the reality of someone's faith in the divine presence. It would be counterproductive to engage in Ignatian Spiritual Exercises if we have no awareness or desire to encounter the divine, the Holy One. If our understanding of everything about ourselves and the world around us is mechanical, with little invitation or space for God, then we might find meditation practice more fitting than the Christian Spiritual Practices, including the Spiritual Exercises of Ignatius focused on here.

The entire Spiritual Exercises are based on three interlocked parts:

1. Experience: Our experience of the Spiritual Exercises will become the bricks and mortar of the edifice we will be constructing. The Exercises are not merely our experiences. They require action and are masterfully designed to help us develop our uniquely authentic and concrete path of living.

2. Practice: The practice will help us to enlarge personal awareness of God in our lives. It also enables us to organize our living in an authentic way suitable to our physicality, our personality, and our affectivity. Let us call it a path of life to be walked on. We will also discover an essential dimension of the Spiritual Exercises, namely, that they provide a way of life based upon a set of practices that are lived within the tradition of a healthy Christian community.

3. Daily Examen: In the practice of Daily Examen, Ignatius will introduce us to a way of being generous with gratefulness and faithfulness in newly discovered ways that result from living as a follower of Jesus.

In addition to these interlocked parts of the Spiritual Exercises, we will also be introduced to the Principle and

Foundation and the five interconnected movements of the entire edifice that Ignatius designed for us:

- The Principle and Foundation: This invites us to radical **openness** of our hearts and calls us to spiritual freedom, leaving behind disordered attachments and our habitual compulsions.

- The First Movement: This invites us to become aware of personal **brokenness** and the deliberate ways in which we harm ourselves, others, and the environment, through destructive or even intentionally sinful behaviors.

- The Second Movement: This places us in a direct line to **encounter** the life of Jesus of Nazareth and personally Jesus as Christ, as the beginning and the end, the Alpha and the Omega, of our lives and all of creation.

- The Third Movement: This movement challenges us to realistically **accept** suffering as a part and parcel of living and loving as in the passion of Christ. It invites us to clarify our values and start discerning their application for our lifestyle.

- The Fourth Movement: This movement places us at the feet of the risen Christ and prepares us to **receive** his life-giving Breath that anoints us for an awakened life of service.

- The Fifth Movement: This allows us to explore concrete ways for **becoming** a loving presence in the world, not only with words but with specific behavioral practices of justice and mercy.

We will also discover throughout the Spiritual Exercises that there are Spiritual Laws in the universe, which include love, kindness, compassion, empathy, altruism, contentment, cooperation, forgiveness, and many more. The consequence of violating these laws is an erosion of the value of human beings and the whole of creation as it is observed in profound disparity between those that "have" and those who "do not have" even the most necessary means for human life with dignity.

The Ignatian Spiritual Exercises invite us to find time for daily prayer, which is an intimate relationship with the divine mystery that Ignatius refers to as the Divine Majesty, Loving God, Father of our Lord Jesus Christ, and whom many of us like to name the Holy One. To foster this intimate relationship with God, we need to allocate time daily to pray.

The Ignatian God is a God of life and a God who desires to be in relationship with you and me and with us. The Ignatian God is a God of generosity and compassion, inviting us always to become authentic and to fully embrace this authenticity as well as a life full of magnanimity for ourselves and for others within the context of our present situations. Ignatius believes that we are to be the best of ourselves, and that God provides us with grace to accomplish that. As we begin the experience and the practice of Ignatian Spiritual Exercises, keep in mind always that becoming authentic and experiencing a flourishing life of meaningful possibilities is our birthright.

Seedlings

One day a neighbor observed Michelangelo rolling a jagged boulder up the street and onto his front step. When the sculptor took out his hammer and chisel and began to strike the boulder, the neighbor was overcome by curiosity. He crossed the street and asked, "What are you doing hammering on that boulder?" To which Michelangelo responded, "There's an angel inside and I'm trying to let it out!"

Unknown author, as told by a friend

•

"Those who live the Exercises in an authentic way experience the attraction and the appeal of God, and return renewed, transformed in ordinary life, in ministry, in daily relationships, bringing with them the fragrance of Christ."

Pope Francis, the Bishop of Rome

•

A six- year-old Scottish girl named Lulu wrote a letter to God: "To God, how did you get invented?" Upon receiving the letter, Archbishop Rowan Williams responded to her:

Dear Lulu,

Your dad has sent on your letter and asked if I have any answers. It's a difficult one! But I think God might reply a bit like this:

"Dear Lulu,

Nobody invented me, but lots of people discovered me and were quite surprised. They discovered me when they looked around at the world and thought it was really beautiful or really mysterious and wondered where it came from. They discovered me when they were very quiet on their own and felt a sort of peace and love they hadn't expected. Then they invented ideas about me, some of them sensible and some of them not very sensible. From time to time I sent them some hints, especially in the life of Jesus, to help them get closer to what I'm really like. But there was nothing and nobody around before me to invent me. Rather like somebody who writes a story in a book, I started making up the story of the world and eventually invented human beings like you who could ask me awkward questions!"

And then he'd send you lots of love and sign off. I know he doesn't usually write letters, so I have to do the best I can on his behalf. Lots of love from me, too.

+Archbishop Rowan

Rowan Williams, 104th Archbishop of Canterbury

LOOKING FOR PRINCIPLE AND FOUNDATION

The Principle and Foundation precedes the Spiritual Exercises proper (Haight, R. 2012).[1]There are Five Spiritual Movements within the Spiritual Exercises, and the Principle and Foundation and the Five Movements together create a unique whole. An epigenetic quality exists between the Principle and Foundation and the Spiritual Movements; one part builds upon the next. Indeed, each part of the Spiritual Exercises has a distinct quality about itself and

---

Haight, R. (2012). Christian Spirituality for Seekers: Reflections on the Spiritual Exercises of Ignatius Loyola, Orbis Books: New York, p. 35

provides the necessary stepping blocks to prepare for the next. Said another way, each movement has an expansive effect, readying the person to proceed in the Spiritual Exercises. At some point, it becomes clear that the Principle and Foundation and the Movements, while separate, also are organically interconnected components of the Ignatian Exercises for an awakening life of discipleship.

Ignatius applies specific Christian anthropology throughout his Spiritual Exercises—God has created us good and wonderful. "And God saw everything that he had made, and behold, it was very good. And there was evening and there was morning, the sixth day" (Genesis 1:31). While part of human behavior is behavior in the direction of sin, there is also redemption and grace. Christian love practiced with justice and mercy is the answer in action. Ignatius uses these basic Christian anthropological principles to ground us in a foundation constructed upon a single-minded purpose: God wants life for us, abundant life and is eager to encounter us on this journey of loving justly with mercy! "He has told you, O man, what is good; And what does the LORD require of you, but to do justice, to love kindness, and to walk humbly with your God?" (Micah 6:8). Each and every one of our lives has purpose no matter how big or small. Our living is filled with meaningful possibilities to be discovered and lived out in the realities of here and now.

Building a house of any size and of any shape requires understanding of many architectural principles that are expressed in the architectural design itself. If we lack the skills for designing our intended project, we turn to an architect who is gifted in such talent and ability.

The selected architect, we hope, takes time and listens carefully to our desires. He asks many questions of us to glean a sense of our desired abode, including the very minute details. Of course, he also wants to know what kinds of resources we have and what the overall purpose is of the house we desire to construct.

Any design created by our architect will certainly include a detailed plan for a foundation that has the strength and stability to support our desired house, a base upon which everything will be built. The foundations will be in direct proportion to the size of the house and the materials used. The design will also incorporate protection from outside forces, such as winds and storms.

In the case of the Spiritual Exercises, Ignatius Loyola becomes like the architect we have hired to direct us on our unique journey to awakening, to the building of our intended spiritual house. He does not leave us without personal companionship on this journey. We are encouraged to have our Spiritual Directors or Spiritual Companions serve as intimate guides. God, in cooperation with each one of us, guides us to build the house of our personal spiritual awakenings in Christ Jesus. Psalm 127 beautifully expresses: Unless the Lord builds the house, those who build it labor in vain.

Ignatian Spiritual Exercises begin with what Ignatius calls a foundational statement: You are here, in this historical time and this specific space, with your little life. The question that follows is regarding the reason for you being here with all the gifts and limitations you are experiencing. What is your purpose for being here? Ignatius places before us his answer: we are created to praise, reverence, and serve God our Lord. In doing this, we live life with a spiritual abundance of inner freedom and a sense of choosing, making decisions and elections. This means that we choose well for ourselves and for those with whom we are in relationship. This kind of living well will alter us interiorly, compelling us to act as agents of change to the structures around us that might need restoring for the betterment of all.

The Spiritual Exercises will open us up to discerning any current structures in our life that imprison and oppress us or any of God's creation, and toward building a life suffused with meaning. In such a way, Ignatius proposes, we gradually move toward the experience of becoming fully alive and fully authentic and open to flourishing living. In doing so, Ignatius suggests, we "save our souls." Again, we need not be alone on this journey of awakening; a Spiritual Director or a Spiritual Companion will and can assist in this discerning process. "What we are destined for in Christ and the communion of saints is beyond what most can begin to imagine (Owens, B., 2015).[2]

Placed before us at this point of the Exercises, is the answer Ignatius gave acceptable? Are we open to considering and accepting as our own the Ignatian answer about the purpose of our human existence, to praise, reverence, and serve God?

Would we be willing to develop our own unique and personal statement of purpose? Would we be willing at this point to initiate a "Personal Statement of Christian Spiritual Identity?" Take a piece of paper and start writing

---

Owens, B. (2015). *More than you can Imagine: On our becoming divine.* Liturgical Press. Collegeville, Minnesota

your own Christian Spiritual Identity Statement now before you continue further reading.

The Ignatian foundational suggestion of purpose at the beginning of the Spiritual Exercises is intentional. He answers his own question first, promptly, and then builds on giving his own answers: everything that we encounter in life, from relationships to things and persons, is given to us to help us attain the very end for which we are created, namely "to praise, reverence, and serve God our Lord," not only now but forever, in everything we do and in everything that we are (Owens, B. 2015). The reign of God is in our midst now and will be forever.

The God that Ignatius desires for us to encounter in the Spiritual Exercises is a living God of Jesus, of Abraham and Moses. This God is generous who never allows Oneself to be outdone with generosity. The Exulted song of the Easter Vigil proclaims when it states, "This is the night, when all who believe in Christ are delivered from the gloom of sin, and are restored to grace and holiness of life. This is the night, when Christ broke the bonds of death and hell, and rose victorious from the grave."

Before we begin, we are asked to remind ourselves of the following: (1) to become **aware** of the quality of our personal **honesty**; (2) to **recognize** the need for **openness** in the discernment process; and (3) to **strengthen** our **willingness** to take steps to live authentically within the context of our situation with personal values that are in harmony with the Gospel values.

Seedlings

If the following statements appeals to you, place them in your heart and ponder their inner meaning. This will cause their inner truth to germinate and grow.

Behold God beholding you... and smiling.

Anthony de Mello, SJ

•

The world is charged with the grandeur of God.

It will flame out, like shining from shook foil;

It gathers to a greatness, like the ooze of oil

Crushed. Why do men then now not reck his rod?

Generations have trod, have trod, have trod;

And all is seared with trade; bleared, smeared with toil;

And wears man's smudge and
shares man's smell: the soil

Is bare now, nor can foot feel, being shod.

And for all this, nature is never spent;

There lives the dearest freshness deep down things;

And though the last lights off the black West went

Oh, morning, at the brown brink eastward, springs -

Because the Holy Ghost over the bent

World broods with warm breast
and with ah! Bright wings.

Gerald Manley Hopkins, S.J.

•

The goal of our life is to live with God now and forever.

God, who loves us, gave us life.

Our own response of love allows God's
life to flow into us without limit.

In everyday life, then, we must
hold ourselves in balance...

Our only desire and our one choice should be this:

I want and I choose what better leads

to God's deepening God's life in me.

Ignatius Loyola

*As paraphrased by David L. Flaming, S.J.

•

Poems and quotations taken from *Praying with Jesuits*, Edited by Michael Harter, S.J.

Harter, M., Editor (1993) *Heart on Fire: Praying with Jesuits*. Chicago: Loyola Press

Scripture:	Psalm 46:10	Be still and know that I am God!
	Isaiah 40:27-31	Comfort for God's People
	Psalm 127	Unless the Lord builds the house
	Matthew 8:23-27	Jesus Calms a Storm

Questions: Who am I? Why am I here?

Practice: Openness to encounter personal spiritual freedom and clarity of purpose!

Ritual: Fifteen minutes daily awareness of God's Presence!

Grace: Spiritual freedom!

Prayerful reflection...

Dear God, I ask what spiritual freedom is? I understand affectively and intellectually and in my physicality that I am your creation. I am in relationships with all your creation, with myself and most of all with you, my God and my Lord. I have bound responsibilities to all these relationships. I have created some of these relationships by my own choosing and some of them have been imposed on me. I realize that I am bound by the given laws of my culture, religious affiliation and personal developments. I am willing to explore all my relationships and examine how they have shaped me. I am not the same person today that I was yesterday.

I thank you for the enormous gift of freedom. The gift of freedom is to make choices. It is an awesome gift that you have given me. I know that I am not free from situations that either I have created or that have been imposed upon me by specific circumstances. I am free, however, to make choices in whatever the given situation might be today. I am not always able to change the situations. I do have an option to choose an attitude toward the given condition. Nobody controls my inner feelings or my inner thoughts. I do. If nothing else, I find areas of freedom when I am willing to make a stand toward the given situation.

Ignatius is inviting me to consider the degrees of freedom that I have about my material possessions, intellectual gifts or liabilities, my physical and emotional health, and my intimate relationships like my partner, my spouse and my children. He is asking me to examine the areas where I could invest of myself, keeping in mind the single purpose of my life and living.

I am called today to examine my relationships with my past. I realize that nothing can be changed regarding my past except for the freedom to choose gratitude for accomplishments and ask for forgiveness for any harm that I have caused anyone including any of God's creation. When appropriate, I choose to make restorations in order to be the instrument of your reconciliation and peace.

I sense that, now, I am more willing to be open to listening to the promptings of your Holy Breath to guide me to the sense of wholeness that comes from deep connection with you.

Holy God! Holy and Mighty! Holy Immortal One!
Have Mercy upon me!

THE FIRST MOVEMENT

The First Movement of the Spiritual Exercises disposes a person to becoming aware of the reality of human brokenness and of human abilities to behave in evil ways. It is during this movement that we realize our potential for personal and communal destructiveness. Theologians call this reality a sin. It is personal when we intentionally behave in the direction of harming ourselves or others or God's creation. It is communal when we participate intentionally in societal structures that destroy the well-being and the very dignity of people or natural resources.

Remember, there is no concept of sin in social sciences or hardcore sciences. There are only observations and gathering of data that support or do not support hypothetical positions. The case in point is the present day human destructiveness contributing in a large extent to climate change. Another example is the incredible discrepancy between the rich and the poor. The misery and the inhumane poverty besetting refugees and other large masses of human beings in many countries is best understood as injustice. Speaking in theological terms, it is human sinful behaviors that are at the root of this misery, as I have observed over time.

We remember during this first movement of the Spiritual Exercises the verse from the Book of Genesis that says: "And God saw everything that he had made, and behold, it was very good. And there was evening and there was morning, the sixth day" (Gen 1:31). It might be helpful to recall the gifted spiritual writer of our time, Mathew Fox,[3] who reminds us in his book entitled *Creation Spirituality: Liberating Gifts for the Peoples of the Earth*, that honoring all creation as Original Blessing could help us understand our sinfulness:

> "Creation Spirituality integrates the wisdom of Eastern and Western and global indigenous cultures, with emerging scientific understanding of the universe, and the passion of creativity. It is both a tradition and a movement, celebrated by mystics and agents of social change from every age and

---

Fox, M. (1991). *Creation Spirituality: Liberating Gifts for the Peoples of the Earth.* San Francisco: Harper

Fox, M. (1983). *Original Blessing:* A Primer of Creation Spirituality. Santa Fe, NM: Bear

> culture. It is also the tradition of the historical Jesus himself since it is the wisdom tradition of Israel."

Another eminent spiritual writer of our time, Kathleen Fisher,[4] in her book *Loving Creation: Christian Spirituality, Earth Centered and Just* (2009) makes a strong statement about our brokenness and sinfulness despite our great giftedness:

> "First, we mastered fire, air, water, and atomic power, and now with technological and scientific advances; the consequences of our domination appear to have no limits.
>
> But the consequences of this domination approach to nature have become clear. Like cancer, uncontrolled mastery metastasizes, poisoning and depleting its host. Recognition of the price domination exacts has contributed to a search for new understanding of the divine spark that defines us."

The Book of Common Prayer helps us to consider sin as the intentional seeking of our personal interests only (BCP p.848). Since we are inter-relational beings, we often forget others, or we intentionally act in the direction of me, myself and I. In psychological sciences, it is called malignant narcissism. In spirituality and religion, it is called sin. These behaviors distort not only the relationship with the Holy One, but also our relationships with others, including the way we relate to all of creation.

Ignatius Loyola invites us during this First Movement to look at our distorted view of relating. He asks us to consider

---

Fisher, K. (2009). *Loving Creation: Christian Spirituality, Earth Centered and Just.* New Jersey: Paulist Press. p.3

and examine the very root sin that is unique to each one of us. What is meant by root sin is the patterns within that bind us and make us less free or even destructive of our very true sense of self. In such a way, our false sense of self dominates and creates a life of its own, however illusory.

During this movement we beg for the necessary grace to become aware of our destructive patterns dominated by the false self. We ask the Holy One to reveal to us what binds us and makes us less free to respond to the call of our Baptismal Covenant (BCP p.304). Using the words of the Baptismal Covenant, we pause for a moment and examine personal awareness of the quality of our relating:

> "Will you continue in the apostles' teaching and fellowship, in the breaking of bread, and in the prayers? I will, with God's Help.
>
> Will you persevere in resisting evil, and whenever you fall into sin, repent and return to the Lord? I will, with God's help.
>
> Will you proclaim by word and example the Good News of God in Christ? I will, with God's help.
>
> Will you seek and serve Christ in all persons, loving your neighbor as yourself? I will, with God's help."

The final Baptismal promise, we are asked to examine relates to the dignity of every human being. We are asked by a presiding priest the following:

> Will you strive for justice and peace among all people, and respect the dignity of every human being? I will, with God's help."

After renewing our Baptismal Covent, the question we turn to now is the question related to our willingness to become closer followers of Jesus. To become a follower of Jesus means to become a Christ's presence in the world. This means to organize our lives in a way that resembles the values and behaviors of our Baptismal Covenant, our Baptismal Promises.

In order for our Baptismal Promises to be real in the real world, we have to undergo and enter into our personal conversion process that gradually leads to transformation of our behaviors. Some readers might prefer the word transformation instead of conversion. In any case, whatever word you prefer to engage, the process of conversion is based on confrontation with parts of ourselves that do not resemble the values of the Baptismal Covenant. We ask ourselves the following questions:

1. Whether our affectivity has been adequately developed and is commensurate with our biological age to inform our ethical/moral behaviors.

2. Whether our intellectual abilities have been adequately sharpened to inform our religious/ spiritual sensibilities and behaviors.

The outline of the Baptismal Covenant provides us with practical behaviors that are based on and flow from our personal way of being a follower of Jesus. My affectivity has matured and is responding authentically to the demands of life and living; my moral/ethical and intellectual abilities have been sharpened to the best of my abilities; my religious/spiritual as well as socio-political behaviors all flow from the awareness of my Baptismal Covenant.

Christian theologians call this process of confrontations with the various parts of myself the conversion process. What this conversion process means to theologians is that an internal shift has occurred within a person. It is a shift from one way of thinking, feeling, and behaving to the Baptismal Covenant way of being in the world. Psychologically speaking, we call this process individuation or maturation.

Psychologists remind us, however, that all of us are somewhere on the continuum between immature to mature, childish to individuated, unhealthy to healthy, reactive to balanced. The more integrated we are, the more willing we are to confront various parts of ourselves in order to live our personal Baptismal Covenant in the real world.

We are invited to conduct a rigorous inventory of our lives by self-examination during the First Movement of the Spiritual Exercises, and to commit to the process of living out the Baptismal Covenant. Conducting this self-examination, we come to an awareness of our root sin and our fixation on it. A helpful guide is found in the Book of Common Prayer[5](BCP p. 267) using the Liturgy of Ash Wednesday, Litany of Penance.

Ignatius Loyola invites us at this point to find courage and confess our blunders, destructive patterns of behaving, and our avoidance or attempts to escape the necessity of conversion. Once we are aware of our patterns that do not give life but rather are destructive, it might be appropriate to ritualize it by using the Reconciliation of a Penitent

---

The Book of Common Prayer According to the use of the Episcopal Church: New York: The Church Hymnal Corporation, p.304 and 305.

Ritual (BCP, p. 447) with a priest. Other times the general form of reconciliation might be sufficient by participating in the Service of the Holy Eucharist, the Mass.

To deepen our awareness of sinful patterns as well as healthy ways of relating, the Enneagram Personality Types system also might prove to be helpful. There are websites offering Enneagram Questionnaires and professional tests to assist us on this journey including Rohr, R. and Ebert, A. (1992),[6]and www.9types.com.

Rohr, R. and Ebert, A. (1992). *Experiencing the Enneagram.* New York: Crossroad

Riso, D.R. and Hudson, R. (1999). *The Wisdom of the Enneagram: The Complete Guide to Psychological and Spiritual Growth for the Nine Personality Types.* New York: Bantam Books

Seedlings

Place the following short sentences in your heart and ponder on their inner meaning. This could cause their inner truth to germinate and grow. Do not force them open with your mind. That would only kill the seed. Sow where the soil is rich. Sow it in your heart. Give them time:

You do not

have

to change

for God

to love

you.

Now, pause prayerfully and experience the above statement. After a needed pause, when ready, make the following statement:

Be grateful

for your sins.

They are carriers

of grace.

Again, paying attention to your breath, make the following statement:

Say goodbye

to golden yesterdays

or your heart

will never learn

to love

the present.

Anthony de Mello, S.J.

•

There is a Chinese folktale about two large pots. One pot was perfect. The other one was cracked. When the water bearer filled them with water and carried them along the path to the house of his master, the cracked pot delivered only a portion of water. After a while the cracked pot felt shame and frequently apologized for his cracked broken side. Only after the water bearer showed him how he cleverly used the cracked pot's broken side by watering flowers on the way, did the cracked pot start accepting his broken side. "For two years I have been able to pick these beautiful flowers to decorate my master's house. Without you being just the way, you are, my master's house would not have these beautiful flowers."

Each of us has our own unique flaws and sins. Each of us has unique gifts and talents. We are all beautiful pots. Some of us are broken and have cracks in our sides. Most of us have limitations and fall somewhere on the continuum between whole and broken. It is our gifts but also the cracks and flaws and sins we each have that make our living together meaningful and rewarding. We are all necessary parts of one Body of Christ. As Apostle Paul said: The eye cannot say to the hand, "I have no need of you," nor again the head to the feet, "I have no need of you" (1 Corinthians 12:21). Whatever our brokenness, we are all part of one another.

•

Repentance reaches fullness when you are
brought to gratitude for your sins.

Anthony de Mello, S.J.

•

---

https://www.uexpress.com/tell-me-a-story/2011/1.23/the-cracked-pot-a-chinese-folktale

Scripture:	John 5:1-9	The healing at the pool
Luke	6:36-38	Judging and condemning yourself and others
Luke	15:11-32	The Parable of two sons or two daughters

Questions: What do I want? Am I willing to engage in the process of personal conversions or transformation?

Practice: Liturgical Rites of God's forgiveness and loving embrace.

Reconciliation of a Penitent, Book of Common Prayer p. 449

Grace: Courage, Gratitude and a personal experience of God's Mercy and God's Hope

Prayerful reflection...

Holy God! Holy and Mighty! Holy Immortal One! Have Mercy on us! Paul the Apostle said it best for us: "For what I am doing, I do not understand; for I am not practicing what I would like to do, but I am doing the very thing I hate" (Romans 7:15).

My Lord and my God! There is this tension inside of us. We can be sometimes like saints and some other times like sinners. We find ourselves in situations and we do not care about anything or anyone. Sometimes we feel so comfortable and other times we feel very uncomfortable and insecure and not safe. Keep us close to you so that this tension between a saint and a sinner, being peaceful and being turbulent, being perfect and being imperfect, being generous and being self-centered, be always in a healthy balance of our baptismal values.

Give us your grace of courage to recognize our vulnerabilities and ask for support from those who love us and care for us to contain our sinfulness. Help us to hear the words of Chief Seattle of the Suquamish Native Americans when he says: "Humankind did not weave the web of life. Whatever we do to the web we do to ourselves." Yes, dear Lord, we desire to consistently live out the values of the Gospels as expressed in our personal Baptismal Covenant with you. Make us an instrument of your Peace! You are the one who nourishes our souls when our roots are dry and desolate, even when we feel broken with our cynicism. We beg you, with the words of Gerard Manley Hopkins, "Mine, O thou Lord of Life, send my roots rain."

Amen

IGNATIAN WAY OF PRAYING

Before entering the formal prayer time, select an appropriate passage from the Scriptures and read it aloud or silently. The selected passage also could be from other resources that you find calling you into prayer.

1. Place yourself mindfully in **God's all-embracing presence**. Breathe in and breathe out, resting in the awareness of God's presence.

2. Gradually call to awareness your desires. Sort out your desires from trivial to most important. Name them and play with them until you **reach the deepest and most authentic desires** of your present life context.

3. When ready, engage **imagination** using a selected passage from the Scriptures or any reading material that could lend itself to creating rich scenes for spiritual awakenings.

4. Involve yourself in **conversation** with one person or another in the scene that draws your interest or curiosity. You may feel drawn

to Jesus or Peter or Mary or someone else, depending on your selected reading, like Mahatma Gandhi or Dietrich Bonhoeffer or Hildegard, etc. Make your conversation as real as possible and as personal as you desire. Remember that "growth in relationship with God occurs through mutual self-revelation," Conroy, M. (1993).

What Ignatius means by conversation (colloquy) is the intimate and personal conversation between the Holy One and me, between Jesus and me, between the Holy Spirit and me, and so on. As with all conversations, Ignatian Colloquy goes both ways. I say something to Jesus and then I give Jesus time to say something back to me. It is not a debate. It is a conversation of the heart.

5. Choose a **particular action,** a specific behavior that you desire to practice today. The particular action or behavior that you choose is always in harmony with the Baptismal Covenant based on the Gospel values.

6. **Close the time of prayer:** Glory be to the Father and to the Son and to the Holy Spirit. As it was in the beginning is now and ever shall be. Amen

---

Conroy, M. (1993). *The Discerning Heart: Discovering a Personal God.* Chicago. Loyola Press. p. 62.

DAILY EXAMEN

A great way to end the day in prayer is to just relax and look back at the day for the Holy One's presence in whatever occurred. Review your feelings, sensations and thoughts of the day.

More than 400 years ago, Ignatius Loyola encouraged prayer-filled mindfulness by proposing what has been called the Daily Examen. The Examen is a technique of prayerful reflection on the events of the day to detect the Holy One's presence and to discern how the Holy Breath of Jesus might be creating a direction for us in this very moment. The following steps are suggestions to conduct the Daily Examen:

1. **Become aware of God's presence.** Immersed in the awareness of the Holy One's presence, we go through the day and we notice our confusions, a blur, a jumble, a muddle or maybe brighter emotions of peacefulness, joy, and hopefulness. We ask the Holy One to bring clarity and understanding.

2. **Review the day with gratitude.** Gratitude is the foundation of our relationship with God.

We walk through our day in the presence of the Holy One and intentionally notice the day's joys and delights, focusing on the day's gifts. We look at the work we did, the people we interacted with. What did we receive from these people? What did we give them? We pay attention to small things—the food we ate, the sights we saw, and other seemingly small pleasures. The Holy One is in the details.

3. **Pay attention to your emotions.** One of Ignatius's great insights was that we detect the presence of the Spirit of the Holy One in the movements of our emotions. We recall and reflect on the feelings we experienced during the day. Boredom? Elation? Resentment? Compassion? Anger? Confidence? What is the Holy One saying through these feelings?

   The Holy one will also show us some ways that we fell short. We make note of these unhealed emotions and how these emotions have harmed us or have harmed others. But we also look with openness for other implications. Does a feeling of frustration perhaps mean that the Holy One might be nudging us to consider a new direction in some area of the way our life is structured? We may be concerned about someone or something in a disorderly attached way, or perhaps our concerns are suggesting that we should reach out to our friend in some healing way.

4. **Choose one feature of the day and pray from it.** Ask the Holy Breath, the Holy Spirit to

direct you to something during the day that is particularly important. It may involve a feeling, positive or negative. It may be a significant encounter with another person or a vivid moment of pleasure or peace. Or it may be something that seems rather insignificant. We look at it. We bring it into prayer and pray about it. We allow the prayer to arise spontaneously from our hearts. We move with the flow of our emotions, whether it be intercession, praise, repentance, gratitude, or adoration.

5. **Look toward tomorrow.** We ask the Holy One to give us light for tomorrow's new possibilities. We pay attention to feelings that surface as we survey what's coming up tomorrow. Are we doubtful? Cheerful? Apprehensive? Full of delighted anticipation? We allow these feelings to turn into prayer. We seek God's guidance. We ask the Holy One for help and understanding. We pray for the grace of hopefulness.

Ignatius encouraged people to **talk to Jesus like a most special friend**. The Daily Examen invites us into this conversation with Jesus. We ask forgiveness for our destructive behaviors. We ask for the Holy One's protection and help. We ask for the Holy One's wisdom about the questions we have and the problems we face. We do all of this in the spirit of gratitude. Our lives are a gift, and they are adorned with gifts from the Holy One.

We end the Daily Examen with the Our Father or Glory be to the Father and to the Son and to the Holy Spirit...

Amen

ON BECOMING SPIRITUAL COMPANIONS

One of the practical tools for journeying to an awakened Christian discipleship is to engage in regular spiritual direction or regular spiritual companionship. This practice could prove to help us in assisting the unfolding of our personal Baptismal Covenant and our own ongoing personal transformations. It is the integrally converted Christian who is willing to stand on an ongoing basis in complete openness to every impulse of the Spirit of God, the Holy Breath. We all are in an ongoing transformation process throughout our life span, always open to the promptings of the Holy Breath of the Father and the Son.

Ignatius suggests that the skillful art of spiritual direction or spiritual companionship is to be engaged in with single-hearted intention, which is to discern the workings of God's Spirit in everything we do and everything we experience. **The central task, therefore, for either the spiritual director or the spiritual companion is to facilitate the awareness of God's work in the one who is undergoing the Spiritual Exercises.** The spiritual companion must keep his or her projections, prejudices, and beliefs from interfering in the work that God is doing here and now with the person we are shepherding to a gradual life of discipleship by using the process of the Ignatian Spiritual Exercises.

The following is an outline for spiritual companionship time. The spiritual companions take turns in exchanging the roles of a sharer and a listener. A *fifteen-minute time* allotment for each is suggested.

Steps to follow for the one who shares or for the one who listens:

- **Clarify the task** with your companion by saying the following in your own words; e.g., for the next fifteen minutes one of us will share and the other one will listen, actively, without interrupting what is being shared. If needed to better understand what is being shared, a simple question may be asked. There will be time for feedback and conversation later. After that, we will change our roles. Who is going to be the listener first? Who is going to be the sharer first?

- **Place ourselves in an awareness of God's Presence;** e.g., we focus attention on breathing in and breathing out and each one of us says internally and silently, "Spirit of the Living God, you are our guide and our light. Give us freedom to discern the workings of your grace during this time together."

- **Verbalize to your companion the personal experiences of the inner workings of God's**

Spirit while involved in prayer time. Describe your feelings, thoughts, and sensations to the best of your abilities.

- **Verbalize specifically your experiences of Consolations and Desolations.**

- **Share behavioral outcomes,** movements toward actions that follow your prayer time.

- **Listen attentively and with open heart and either clarify observations or process questions** that your spiritual companion places before you.

- **Converse with genuine kindness and mutual openness about the experiences of your prayer time.** When negative feelings flare up, name them and process them with your spiritual companion, always mindful that God is working in everything for the benefit of each one of us.

THE SECOND MOVEMENT

The Second Movement aims at assisting us in encountering the human face of God, Jesus of Nazareth, from the moment of his birth and throughout his public ministry. Beginning with the narrative of his birth, it places Mary and Joseph and the shepherds and the three wise people from the East at the center of the story and uses the reality of the hurting and broken world as the context. These are the theological legends of the Gospels, attempting to convey the truths of our uniquely Christian story.

Our concentration during this movement is on Jesus. As Tom Hart[7] invites us in his book, *To Know and Follow Jesus: Contemporary Christology* (1984), it is Jesus who lived for God; it is Jesus who lived for others; it is Jesus who is the Sacrament of God's Presence, Love, and Power; it is Jesus who is free. This is who Jesus is for us as we encounter him during this Second Movement toward awakening our life of discipleship. We will encounter and prayerfully consider the teachings of Jesus: the love of God; love of neighbor; simplicity of life; and, in particular, Jesus' attitude toward suffering.

The baptism of Jesus in the river Jordan serves as the initiation moment into Jesus' public ministry. Our baptism initiates each one of us into our own public ministry as followers of Jesus.

Bishop Dan Edwards, the retired Bishop of the Episcopal Diocese of Nevada, helps us with his words and introduces us into the meaning of the Baptism of Jesus as well as our own baptism:

> "We liturgical Christians perform rituals, symbolic actions that mean something – though we are not precisely certain what they mean.
>
> We are wise to keep our hearts and minds open about the meaning because rituals are a kind of dance with God in which God leads and we follow.

Hart, T. (1984). *To Know and Follow Jesus: Contemporary Christology.* New Jersey: Paulist Press, p.24

Hart, T. (1999). *Spiritual Quest: A Guide to the Changing Landscape.* New Jersey: Paulist Press, p. 71

Even if we know what we mean, God may have something else—or something more—in mind.

John probably intended Baptism to mean a cleansing from sin. But after Jesus stepped out of the river, something unexpected happened with a different meaning.

He was praying, perhaps asking God what his baptism was about, when the sky opened, the Holy Spirit descended on him, and a voice from heaven said, "You are my Son, the beloved."

So, what does this suggest is going on in Baptism? It may have something to do with this: I once heard of an old Bishop who had a spiritual practice. At the start of each day he would look in the mirror and say, "Whatever happens this day, I am baptized." His Baptism gave him an assurance he could count on despite all the ups, downs, and sideways vicissitudes of life.

Here's why: The waters of Baptism can represent many things. But one thing they would surely have represented for Jesus was the primordial waters of chaos. Call it entropy or Murphy's Law. It's the way things tend to go wrong. That's what waters stood for in antiquity.

Isaiah says, "When you pass through the waters, I will be with you and the rivers will not overwhelm you."

"Do not fear for I have redeemed you. I have called you by name. You are mine."

Baptism is God saying that to us, "When you pass through the waters, when everything falls apart, I will be with you. . . Fear not for I have redeemed you. You are mine."

Baptism isn't just us talking, God is acting here too. God redeems us. He buys us back from all the world's chaos, all the powers of sin, death, and madness that lay claim to precious human lives. God redeems us from the world and reclaims us as his own.

That's what we can take to heart. No matter what happens, no matter how badly we fail, when we are good and when we are bad, when we are wise and when we are foolish, when we are holy and when we are profane, in the darkness or the light, we are God's.

Blessed Paul said it best: "If God is for us, who can be against us? . . . What shall separate us from the love of Christ? Shall trouble or hardship or persecution or famine or nakedness or danger or sword? No, in all these things we are more than conquerors through him who loved us."

"For I am convinced," Paul said, "that neither death nor life, neither angels nor demons, neither the present nor the future, nor any powers, neither height nor depth nor anything in all creation can separate us from the love of God that is in Christ Jesus Our Lord."

To be claimed by God is to be set free of our burden. The basic existential threat is resolved: we are already justified. We are set free.

That doesn't mean nothing bad will happen. All those threats Paul listed—trouble, hardship, danger, famine, sword—all of that is real and may happen at any time.

Life and death will assuredly happen. But they do not and cannot separate us from our fundamental well-being, the love of God in Christ Jesus Our Lord.

People sweat, lose sleep, spike their blood pressure, and wreck their relationships trying to justify their existence, trying to make themselves okay in God's eyes. But guess what: that's already been done. In our Baptism, God has made it so. God has set us free from bondage to the hopeless task of justifying ourselves, making ourselves righteous and free.

So, what are we, now, to do with our freedom? Once the Holy Spirit comes upon us in Baptism, naming us as God's children, what are we going to do with that freedom? As Mary Oliver asked in her poem *Summer Day*, "Tell me what is it you plan to do with your one wild precious life?"

Well that's exactly what Jesus was wondering after he got the good news, "You are my Son, the Beloved." He was so perplexed about it that he had to spend 40 days out in the desert praying on it. Only after all that prayer did he figure it out. He came back from the desert with the answer.

Now listen carefully because if you call yourself a Christian, his answer is your answer, too. Jesus said: "The Spirit of the Lord is upon me because he has anointed me to proclaim good news to the poor, . . . freedom to the prisoners, recovery of sight to the blind, to set the oppressed free."

In Baptism, God claims us as his own, breaks our chains and gives us "our one wild precious life." We are redeemed. We are okay.

But whether the life we live with that freedom amounts to a hill of beans is still up for grabs. To make our lives as holy as our redeemed souls, we take the next step. We give our lives back to God. That's Confirmation. We take vows to live in the Spirit that sets us free, the Spirit that "proclaim(s) good news to the poor, . . . freedom to the prisoners, recovery of sight to the blind, (and) sets the oppressed free."

We stand up to our God, eye to eye, and promise "to proclaim by word and deed the good news of God in Christ, to seek and serve Christ in all persons, to strive for justice and peace among all people, and respect the dignity of every human being."

If we make those promises without our fingers crossed, it will change our lives, our whole lives, our family lives, our friendships, our politics.

If ten percent of Christians took those vows for what they are, a chance to live a life that counts, we'd do what those first Christians in Acts were accused of doing. We'd turn the world upside down, which Bishop Curry reminds us is really right side up.

Now I'll close with a word of wisdom and a question. The word of wisdom is from Ralph Waldo Emerson. He said:

"The purpose of life is not to be happy. It is to be useful, to be honorable, to be compassionate, to have it make some difference that you have lived and lived well."

I'll leave you with that and Mary Oliver's question:

"What is it you plan to do with your one wild precious life?"

Posted by Bishop Dan's blog at 6:41 PM January 2016

This Second Movement invites us to follow Jesus very closely as he walks and talks, heals and preaches the vision of the "Reign of God" in our midst. As we follow Jesus, we will be noticing gradual awakenings into our own discipleship as the followers of Jesus. We will be experiencing genuine solidarity with all human beings and all of God's creation as we continue our journeys of awakenings in becoming followers of Jesus.

Seedlings

Dreams dissolved

into wander dust.

And so we did

what families do

when confronted

with calamity.

We drew straws.

Shorty lost.

The question is who Shorty is in this poem. It is Jesus? He is the one who came and who comes continuously. As Michael Moynahan, S.J. continues saying:

He came to share

your plight,

your fight,

your night,

And point you

toward tomorrow.

Michael Moynahan, S.J.

•

Scripture:

Isaiah 52:7-10	How beautiful on the mountains...
Luke 2:8:20	The Birth of Jesus
Matthew 3:13-17	The Baptism of Jesus
Matthew 4:11	The Temptations of Jesus
1 Corinthians 9:1-27	The rights of an Apostle

Question:	Who is my God?
Practice:	Fifteen minutes daily prayer following Ignatian Prayer Method.
Ritual:	Engaging in regular Spiritual Companionship and/or Spiritual Direction.
Grace:	Affective, interior and intimate knowledge of Jesus in order to love him more deeply and follow him more closely.

Prayerful Reflection...

We stand before you, dear Lord Jesus. There is this stirring deep within us that makes us desirous of being closer to you. You are our Lord and our God, our Master. We see ourselves in your eyes.

I see you calling me out of the boat of safety and security. I choose to follow you as a close companion. I want to share with you everything that I have. I am counting on you sharing with me everything that you are, my strength and my guide.

We desire to be your disciples and live out in our real daily life your values, your dreams for your people, for this blessed island home, the Earth. Our hearts are set on fire to be your followers. Accept us into your service.

Amen

TWO OPPOSING SETS OF VALUES

We are gradually becoming aware by now, no matter where we are on our journey in the Spiritual Exercises, that we live our lives somewhere on the continuum between two opposing sets of values. On the one hand there are the values of Christ as described by the Gospels. On the other hand, there are the values that are contrary to the values of Christ. They are the values of darkness or in the words of the Gospel of John, the values of the world (John 17, 15-19). These are the two extreme points on the same continuum that we human beings encounter daily and sometimes intensely. Most of us live somewhere on this continuum between the two opposing sets of values. Sometimes with more intensity and other times with less depending on issues we face.

As an example, we are thinking of people who take the Gospel values to their hearts and practice them zealously in daily lives. And then consider people who live in the darkness of extremisms. The news of the beheading of 21 Christian migrant workers in Libya, as reported by Cairo News Agency on February 16, 2015, is just one example of some people being involved with the forces of darkness:

> *Cairo carried out air strikes against Islamic State group targets in Libya on Monday after the jihadists posted a video showing the beheadings of 21 Egyptian Christians.*

Since we accept that we live somewhere on the continuum between the two-opposing set of values, we frequently intellectualize and remain ambivalent by saying to ourselves that living is complex. Nonetheless the tension between the opposing values may be our daily experience. We do the best we are able to do, counting on the grace of God.

During the Second Movement of the Spiritual Exercises, we ask for the grace to know Jesus more intimately, to love him more ardently, so as to follow him more closely.

Now during this contemplation on the Two Standards or Two Opposing Sets of Values, we ask for a special grace: the grace to recognize the false values, the destructive values that destroy and rob human life of its dignity, especially when they appear under the disguise of good.

Seedlings

The very starkness of the images which shape the Christian apocalyptic imagination dramatize the radical character of the choice one must make between values of the Reign of God and the oppressive kingdoms of the world.

Donald Gelpi,[8] S.J. states: "Identification with the victims of human oppression breeds eschatological longing, as the

---

Gelpi, Donald L. (2009). *Encountering Jesus Christ: Rethinking Christological Faith and Commitment.* Milwaukee: Marquette University Press, p.534.

evangelist Luke correctly taught. When Christians identify with the poor, the marginal, and the outcast, when they stand with those who suffer at the hands of the Pilates and Caiphases of this age, when Christians recognize both Christ and themselves crucified in those crucified today, then participation in the passion of Jesus inevitably causes Christian hearts to burst with the cry: Come Lord Jesus! Come, put an end to the sinful powers which crush your people and vindicate the fidelity of those who trust in you."

And Kevin O'Brien,[9]S.J. admonishes us when he says: "It seems like an easy choice. Who wouldn't choose Christ? But as we learned in the First Week of the Exercises, the strategies of darkness are subtle. The voices of darkness begin by seducing us with riches. Such riches can win for us honors and the esteem of others, which we can begin to excessively desire. Fixation on riches and honors develops into self-serving pride, leaving little room for God or anyone else."

Joseph Tetlow,[10]S.J. distills the tactics of the voices of darkness in his personal exclamation:

"Look at all this stuff I have!

leads to

Look at me with all this stuff!

leads to

Look at me!"

O'Brien, Kevin (2011). *The Ignatian Adventure: Experiencing the Spiritual Exercises of Saint Ignatius in Daily Life.* Chicago: Loyola Press, p.168.

Tetlow, Joseph (2008). *Making Choices in Christ: The Foundations of Ignatian Spirituality.* Chicago: Loyola Press, p 95.

The strategy of Christ is the opposite, Tetlow emphasizes. "We embrace the counter-cultural values of spiritual poverty, self-giving, and dignified humility."

•

Scripture:

Matthew 4:1-11	Three Temptations
Luke 4:14:21	Jesus reads from Isaiah

Question:	Are my values in harmony with the Gospel values?
Practice:	Following Jesus more closely...
Ritual:	Sign of the Cross: In the Name of the Father and of the Son and of the Holy Spirit
Grace:	To recognize false values...

NINE TYPES OF PERSONALITIES

We have our personalities. We are not our personalities. We have become our personality as an adaptation to the situations that have shaped us for better or for worse.

We acquire a personality that is partly genetic and partly influenced by environment as a way of coping with life's conflicts.

Become aware and educate yourselves about "my genetics," "my environment," and "my conflicts." Who I am today is a byproduct of many givens as well as our ways of negotiating through them. All of it makes us the unique personality that we have become. It makes us frequently behave in a direction of a false self or neurotic fixations. It also calls us to an intentional living in the direction of the Gospel values that include compassion and loving, forgiving and reconciling. It is the direction of becoming our authentic selves as well as our healthy selves in Christ Jesus, our Lord.

Discovering my true self in the context of my Baptismal Covenant, away from fixations, usually facilitates a personal journey into discipleship as a follower of Jesus. Using

Enneagram,[11] the Nine Personality approach to understand ourselves and others could prove to be helpful. There are many helpful instruments on the enneagram websites to assist you in finding your fixations. The Sacred Enneagram,[12] Finding Your Unique Path to Spiritual Growth written by Christopher Heuertz, could prove to be of a special help.

Beesing, M. and Nogosek,R. and O'Leary, P. (1984). *The Enneagram: A Journey of Self Discovery.* New Jersey: Dimension Books, Inc.

Riso, D.R. and Hudson, R. (1999). *The Wisdom of the Enneagram: The Complete Guide to Psychological and Spiritual Growth for the Nine Personality Types.* New York: Bantam Books

Heuertz, C. (2017). *The Sacred Enneagram: Finding Your Unique Path to Spiritual Growth. Zondervan,* Harper Collins Publishers: Grand Rapids, Michigan

NINE PERSONALITY TYPES IN PRAYER

It is my clinical conviction that the posture we take in prayer is at least colored if not completely imbued by our personality type. Attending to the Enneagram System of personality, I propose that each type adopts a style of prayer that corresponds to our centers of intelligence, namely head or thinking types of prayer (5,6,7), heart or feeling types of prayer (2,3,4), and body, sensation types of prayer (8,9,1). When we recognize our style of praying, then we might be willing to pay attention to inner workings of our unique prayer style that is calling us to recognize the Holy One, the focus of our praying. Some spiritual masters call this paying attention to our inner workings—interior life.

It takes years, a long time to become our personality. Our personality is an important part of our development and it helps us to function in the world. It will therefore take some time to recognize our personality type, accept it as our unique path in life, and open ourselves to transformations. It will also take time to recognize our healthy and our unhealthy ways of praying; i.e., the unhealed places that appear unresolvable and give us feelings of stuck-ness.

The Enneagram system teaches us that we all have compulsive ways of looking at reality. These compulsive ways are also called traps. Being caught in our compulsive personality patterns perpetuates, what Karen Horney calls, the neurotic process. "It is a process of abandoning the real self for an idealized one, of trying to actualize this pseudo-self instead of our given human potential."

Where do the compulsive ways of looking at reality come from? Developmental psychologist Erik Erikson proposed psychosocial stages of human development. He conceptualized that a healthy human is working through unique stages of life as if accomplishing tasks. Each human being, as we work through specific developmental stages, matures epigenetically. This means that each stage builds on previous successful accomplishments. Developmentally, individuals should pass through these stages from infancy to late adulthood and old age in which a special psychological task still remains—ego integrity vs. despair.

I encourage you to explore Erik Erikson psychosocial developmental stages because they can inform you of your own development and how it shapes your prayer life [https://www.learning-theories.com/eriksons-stages-of-development.html].

We humans have a unique ability to refuse to work through developmental stages as suggested by clinical psychology. When we refuse and abort our work on a specific developmental stage, we create compulsions and traps that have specific cognitive, emotional, and sensate distortions.

In spiritual development being aware of our psychosocial development is essential. One supports the other. Our relationship with God, the Holy One, is better understood through the lenses of stage development. It is difficult to trust God when we have been traumatized in the area of trust. William Barry (1994),[13] a spiritual writer of our time relates the following story: “A father puts his five-year-old son Sammy on a ten-foot-high wall. ‘Jump, Sammy, I’ll catch you.’ ‘I am scared.’ ‘Trust your father, Sammy, I’ll catch you.’ Finally, after much cajoling, Sammy jumps and his father steps aside. ‘That’s a lesson for you, Sammy. Never, ever, trust anyone.’ Sammy won’t forget that lesson in a hurry, will he?”

Take time, paper and a pencil and review your history and explore where you might have been hurt that distorts and prevents your individual relationship with God, the Holy One.

The Enneagram system suggests nine such distortions. These distortions create within us a false sense of self as opposed to true sense of self. Some people prefer the language of authentic self and inauthentic self. The Enneagram system could help us to work through our developmental stages and assist us in our prayer life to experience our true or authentic self as invited by Ignatius Loyola in his Spiritual Exercises. In fact, I believe that Ignatian Spiritual Exercises have a single purpose which is to assist us in becoming authentic before ourselves and the Holy One which Jesus revealed to us.

Let us now name specific compulsions or traps of each Enneagram personality type that contribute to the creation of our false, inauthentic or unbalanced self.

Barry, W.A. (1994). *Finding God in all things. Notre Dame*: Ave Maria Press, p.21.

Thinking Types

Type Five: The Investigator and Thinker as well as Observer

The Need to Perceive or Understand to be Capable and Competent

Type Six: The Loyalist but also Devil's Advocate as well as Guardian

The Need to be Sure, Certain, or Secure

Type Seven: The Enthusiast and Generalist as well as Epicure and Dreamer

The Need to Avoid Pain, to be Happy, Satisfied, and find Fulfillment

Body Types

Type Eight: The Challenger and Leader as well as Boss and Confronter

The Need to Constantly Push Against Life to Feel Solid and Alive

Type Nine: The Peacemaker and Mediator as well as Preservationist

The Need to Avoid Conflict and Maintain safe space for Stability and Peace of Mind

Type One: The Reformer and Perfectionist as well as Achiever

The Need to be Perfect, Good, and Virtuous, to Have Integrity

Feeling Types

Type Two: The Helper and Giver

The Need to Feel Loved

Type Three: The Achiever and Status Seeker as well as Performer and Succeeder

The Need to Succeed to Feel Worthwhile, Accepted, and Desirable

Type Four: The Individualist and Artist as well as Tragic Romantic

The Need to be Unique, to find Themselves and Their Significance

If our compulsions and our traps are the bricks and mortar of our false or unbalanced self, the question is what builds our true or balanced self?

The Enneagram teachings could be helpful here. We need to understand the lines between the numbers on the Enneagram and what they symbolize. The lines between each of the types point to Disintegration (unhealthy, compulsive, neurotic, self-sabotage) or Integration (healthy, meaningful, resilient, self-actualization).

The Enneagram theory, therefore, maintains that the lines between the numbers symbolize a move toward integration, an invitation to allow our dominant type and borrow the positive traits of another type. It is observed that the path of disintegration, on the other hand, could be understood as a subconscious self-preservation instinct to prevent an unhealthy person from falling deeper down the hole they feel stuck in.

Let me give you the directions of disintegration first: 1 goes to 4 – 2 – 8 – 5 – 7 – 1; 9 -6 – 3 -9, only to repeat the path of disintegration and falling deeper into the hole again. The path of integration goes into opposite direction: 1 goes to 7 – 5 – 8 – 2 – 4 - 1; 9 – 3 – 6 - 9.

Some researchers of the Enneagram system call directions of disintegration "our responses to stress." Our responses to integration, they call "our invitation to growth." The following diagrams might help us to understand better how the system works in our daily experiences as we respond to stress or as we respond to growth. Find your personality type and follow the arrows of integration or arrows of disintegration on the following diagrams until you become familiar with the journey. Remember, it is a dynamic journey and not the point that we arrive at. The point of arrival is the moment of our death when the journey of this earthy life is complete. Until that moment, we are in process of constant transformations.

It is also important to consider development of Virtues as we talk about the Nine Personality Types in prayer. The Virtues could be considered the unexpected gifts when we are aligned with what is good, true, and beautiful within our identity. Experiencing Virtues in the Enneagram is an experience of the very best of what our hearts were created for. They are fertile soil of our souls for each one of us, uniquely contributing to the world we all desire to live in. The Virtues in the tradition of the Enneagram types are as follows:

Thinking Types

Type Five: Detachment; Silence

Type Six: Courage; Silence

Type Seven: Sobriety; Silence

Body Types

Type Eight: Innocence; Stillness

Type Nine: Action: Stillness

Type One: Serenity, savoring of what is; Stillness

Horney, K. (1950). *Neurosis and Human Growth.* W.W. Norton: New York

Barry, W. A. (1991). *Finding God in All Things.* Ave Maria Press, Notre Dame: Indiana

https://www.enneagraminstitute.com/how-the-enneagram-system-works/

Feeling Types

Type Two: Humility; Solitude

Type Three: Truthfulness, Authenticity; Solitude

Type Four: Equanimity, Emotional Balance, being rooted in the Source of love; Solitude

Head Types in Prayer

Type Five

I place myself in your comforting presence, oh God of my being. I think I am invisible to you, very small! You know that I am so familiar with ambivalence in all relationships. I just hunker down and create my own world of reality and fantasize myself as the best knowledgeable teacher and a professor or some kind of a leader in my own made up world. I love ideas and being someone who has something unusual and insightful to say.

I desire your presence to transform me and give me knowledge to understand and comprehend how this wonderful world you are creating moves and operates.

I do not need much from anyone. I do not depend on social validation. If others agree with my ideas too readily, I fear that my ideas might be too conventional. I desire to be alone and be a burning candle to your glory and praise in my area of specialty. However, with the constant churning of questions in my mind, I surrender to your silent presence that heals me and gives me clarity and inner knowing. You, dear Lord, are the quiet, undisturbed vastness from which everything arises, including all knowledge and creativity.

Teach me, dear Lord, to connect with your creation, especially with people, and keep my clarity of purpose before my eyes.

I will practice today to interact with my colleagues and be open to realize that I am accepted as I am. I will practice an attitude that I am safe in spite of not knowing all the answers.

Amen

Type Six

Your presence, Oh Lord, gives me the security and support I need. I am afraid to be abandoned. To be abandoned means to be separated and left alone. You know that dependency gives me comfort and inner security. My dependency on you gives me inner strength and clarity. The more I dwell in your presence, the more self-affirming and trusting of others I become. Lift my fear of being unable to survive in this world on my own. Your gifts that you have given me are enough for me.

I pray that your presence transforms me to live a committed and loyal life among those I live and interact with. Make me reliable, responsible, and trustworthy. I realize that when I engage your silence, I experience courage and let go of my apprehensions and my suspiciousness.

I will practice today to be sure in myself before your presence and cooperate as an equal with those around me. I will practice letting go of fearful self-doubts and move to self-confidence with tenacious fortitude.

Amen

Type Seven

God of all creativity, Your presence is a true source of love and grace. You, Holy One, offer the completion I seek of all my activities and my strivings. Guide me to my fulfillment which awaits me when I can rest in the calm of your presence.

Despite being practical and engaged in a multitude of projects at any given time, I pray for your guidance to discover the richness of the present moment with you. My mind seeks calm. My mind moves rapidly from one idea to the next. I feel exhilarated by the rush of ideas and by the pleasure of being spontaneous. I prefer broad overviews and the excitement of the initial stages of the creative process to probing a single topic in depth.

I look at You, Jesus, and I see calmness. But my emotions frequently seem to be distant. I avoid my sadness. My body is most content in motion. You have created me with abundant energy. Empty me now of my obsessive planning and all the ideas that overwhelm me. Allow my energy to deepen me, not scatter me. You offer me bountiful gifts, gifts that lead to my wholeness. Oh, Holy One, guide me to my heart, that I may feel not only my joy, but the richness of my sadness. Deep down, I recognize that it is my sadness that I am avoiding; it is limitation I am fearful to encounter. Bring me home to my true self where I find the freedom to be me.

I will practice today and walk on the path toward reverence of myself and of others. I will rest in silence and will dial back my mental preoccupations of what is next.

Amen

Body Types in Prayer

Type Eight

Loving God, I sit here before you aware of your presence in uncomfortable stillness. My thoughts are rumbling, and my feelings are full of fear. I do not want to be harmed or in any way controlled by others or violated in any way. Protect me, loving God. Help me determine my own unique course in my life. Make me comfortable in your presence. May the stillness of my heart open me to your kindness and generosity.

I offer myself to You, loving and magnanimous God. I surrender finally to you despite my fear of letting go. Teach me to transcend my self-interests with generosity and not to bend things to my will. I surrender my need to control situations or people. I surrender myself to you, loving and compassionate God.

I ask You for the gift of genuine freedom that gives birth to simple and more relaxed relationships. I know well that life is not fair and that I am willing to take the heat and do whatever is necessary to protect the people who are under my care. I know deep down in my heart that much of the enduring good in our world has been achieved through determination and struggle.

Open my heart, loving God, to care for those in need. Only when I am in your presence do I admit to myself how much I care about people. I offer you my consent to guide me in letting go of my defenses. No matter how full of rage and shut down I may be, I know I am waiting for the opportunity to contact the world on its own terms by getting in greater contact with my heart and my gentler feelings.

I feel very vulnerable, dear God of all. I am more and more willing to let go of control. I am becoming aware that I am very gradually being liberated from self-reliance and self-assertion. I sense that Your presence is a real warmth to my body as my fears are gradually loosening the grip of my long-term behaviors. I sense that something ennobling is arising out of my surrender to You, the loving and caring God.

Amen

Type Nine

Loving God, your presence fills me with peace that gives me contentment. I am devoted to the quest for internal and external peace for myself and for others. I have such a great yearning for connection with the whole cosmos as well as with other people. I work hard to maintain personal peace of mind. I also work hard to establish peace and harmony in my environment and in the world.

Dear Lord, I do not have a strong sense of my own identity. I am fearful to assert myself against others. This is terrifying to me. I prefer, at my worst, to melt into someone else or quietly follow my idyllic daydreams. I am aware that I idealize others to avoid investing energy in developing myself and my talents. You, Holy One, assure me that investing in myself will not lead me away from others. In fact, I have been noticing that everyone benefits from a stronger, more fully actualized me.

But first, dear Lord, give me grace to process my angers. That feeling of anger is very threatening to me. I want to sense healthy anger in my body. I know that in sensing my healthy anger, I connect with my inner power to act with patience and endurance. I sense I am important. But frequently I debase myself. I feel graceful and powerful when I listen to my healthy anger. Only then, can I be aligned in the service of your Divine will. Real love is frightening to me. You are that Love that I seek.

Today I choose to practice total surrender to You, Oh, Holy One. You are transforming me into this love that is You. I sense that my resistance to my inner journey is melting. I am engaging stillness today to animate this awareness of loving myself. I am taking time today to learn to honor my body and all the aspects of life in order to experience a harmonious world without fear. Make me an instrument of Your peace.

Amen

Type One

Oh, Holy, Loving and All-Embracing God, I am humbly prostrate before you in prayer at this moment. I have learned along the journeying of my life that to be loved, I must be good, and to be good, I must be right. This belief manifests as a continual need to point out errors or better way of doing things. This compels me to debate others about any number of things, from political to psychological, or religious issues of our time. I know that I have many good points to make, but it comes from a deep sense of unhealthy responsibility and feelings of guilt, particularly when things are obviously wrong.

When disenchanted and alienated, I feel that even You, Holy One, do not understand me or appreciate how hard

I am working to make the world a better place. Feelings of envy and resentment become strong and disintegrate into pouting.

I realize, as I sit in silent prayer before You, Loving God, the demands are my own doing. It is I who push myself beyond my own limitations of endurance. No doubt the projects are important, but I need to get better at taking breaks to refresh myself in the gifts of your creation. I am more and more aware that not everything should fall on my shoulders. Others must help even if they do not do as good a job as I expect them to do. Serenity helps me, dear Lord, to accentuate the positive in what others do.

At last it makes me humble to realize that I am not able to get rid of the parts of me that I do not like. If I hold that there is some other way that I am supposed to be, I cannot really be with who and what I am right now.

Teach me, dear Lord, to be consistent and "walk the walk." Integrity is crucial to me. The central principal that I like about myself is a sense of evenhandedness, of wanting other people to be treated fairly. I want to be treated fairly.

I enjoy working hard and making good use of my time. Guide me, dear Lord, to be spontaneous in my instinctive responses to life. I am gradually learning to be affected by reality without needing to tense against it. In doing so, I realize that I am becoming less opinionated and more open to a wider variety of possibilities in myself. There is a sense of curiosity awakening in me, more optimism with appreciation of views differing from my own.

I am afraid of my anger. I fear getting out of control. I am challenged to make peace in my internal war by accepting all parts of myself as they are without condemnation. Give me, Lord, a discerning heart to notice that all things have different qualities. Condemnation includes an emotional reaction that interferes with discernment.

Deep down in my heart, dear Lord, I know in this moment the universe is unfolding exactly as it must. I will practice today what Julian of Norwich beautifully stated, "All is well. Every manner of things will be well."

Amen

Feeling Types in Prayer

Type Two

Merciful and Loving God, I want to feel loved for myself alone. I am unsure whether others would be close to me if I stop being generous and supportive. When someone appreciates my generosity, it does not touch my underlying feelings of worthlessness. Sometimes it feels that people know the hidden agendas of my generosity. I have experienced my friends distancing themselves from me. I am afraid to be rejected.

Teach me, dear Lord, to love genuinely. Give me that love that arises spontaneously when I am truly connected with my heart, my genuine self. When disconnected from my heart, I feel so empty and worthless and my pride covers over all these painful feelings. The more insecure I get, the more I tend to flatter others with the hope that they will appreciate themselves.

Unless certain people say words like "I love you" with a particular tone in their voice, and with a loving look in their eyes, I am fearful, dear Lord, that I am not loved.

This kind of inner insecurity makes me ambivalent to accept even overt signs of affection as evidence of love. I am aware that I miss a lot of love that is offered to me. At worst, I doubt that anyone really does love me.

When I get stressed in my own trap of my personality, I become blunt and forceful and sometime very inappropriately so. Dear Lord, create within me a genuine, loving heart, so that I am not so concerned about what others think of me. I do not need to win over anyone. I know that no matter what I do, I almost always end up displeasing someone.

Holy God, teach me to recognize the affection and good wishes of others, even when they are not in terms that I am familiar with. I am starting to recognize that most people are not as effusive in their feelings as I am, and most are not as naturally inclined to give attention to others as I am.

Most importantly, dear Lord, teach me to develop good boundaries. It will help me to feel for others without becoming entangled in their problems. Teach me, Loving God, to "sit in my own skin" when others are troubled or need something from me.

Today I will practice deeper awareness, dear Lord, and I will allow myself to experience the omnipresence of love. I will be aware that my primary job in life is not to "do good" or to "give" love to anyone, but to be open to the action of love that flows from Your Divine abundance. Having received love, I will be more ready to genuinely share this love with others. Recognizing this essential part about me brings me a tremendous sense of spiritual freedom.

Amen

Type Three

I am restless in solitude and have trouble dwelling in Your presence, Loving and Creative God. Unless I am accomplishing good things, I feel worthless. Unless others think well of me, your presence is not good enough for me.

I need others to think well of me. I am aware that I need attention, encouragement, and affirmation to thrive. I must have success because I am afraid of disappearing into a chasm of emptiness and worthlessness. I am afraid that I am nobody and have no value unless I accomplish things successfully.

I have learned over the course of my life that when I get validated for my achievements, it is not for me but for something I have accomplished. That leaves me empty. I want to hear that I am wonderful! I want to hear that I am pleasing to someone! I want to know that I am appreciated just for me! My successes are far less important to me.

I am tired of lying to myself to keep up my self-esteem and to motivate myself toward greater achievements. I am not a commodity constantly packaging myself for greater accomplishments. I need to reconnect with my heart and grow in authenticity. I am aware that only in this way, revealing my true self with honesty and humility, do I become genuinely content and relaxed in Your presence, dear Lord.

Today, I will affirm my true value as the person that I am, and observe how the center of gravity shifts from outside of me to inside of me. I want to cultivate this feeling of being guided by Your Spirit who speaks to my heart. This is something very new for me, dear Lord. I have never experienced it before. I sense the greatness of Your Spirit within me now. I feel within me the beginning of a new life of love, richness, and wonder.

Amen

Type Four

Loving and compassionate God, I know that I am sensitive, dramatic and temperamental. There is something missing in myself. I believe I lack a clear and stable identity, and would feel more comfortable with a more engaging social persona.

I feel different from others, but I do not want to be alone. I have a deep desire to connect with people who understand me and appreciate me. I desire the easiness and confidence that others seem to enjoy.

Loving God, guide me to let go of feelings from my past. Since I tend to nurse wounds and hold on to negative feelings about those who have hurt me, give me inner strength to release my negative feelings. I do not want to be attached to my longings and disappointments. I want to let them go away from my heart and my memory.

Growing up, I frequently thought that I was mistakenly switched at the hospital. I always felt that I wasn't "seen" by my mother and my dad. I felt like a lost child in my family. I have this uncomfortable feeling within me that there is something profoundly wrong with me. Yet, I know it is not true! I question and say to myself: "If I am not like my parents and I cannot see myself in them, then who am I?"

I have learned that I am not my feelings. I am what I feel! I am getting better with that. I am becoming aware that my feelings always change. I am learning that by allowing the spontaneous arising of my feelings in response to the moment, I can remain well balanced and have a sense of my authentic self. Particularly in my work, I am gradually becoming better at living in the real world of doing things that are meaningful and give me a sense of purpose.

Loving God, I am withdrawing less and less into my internalized self, which is based on idealized qualities that would be virtually impossible for anyone to attain, even with hard work and self-discipline. I am aware that if I give into my fantasy self, I reject myself and my qualities and my capacities.

Today I will pay attention to how my true self, dear Lord, is not a thing with fixed attributes, it is an ever-transforming, and ever-renewing process. A fundamental aspect of my soul is impressibility, which is the ability to be touched and to grow from all my experiences. Today, I will find moments and give myself permission to be touched by life. I know my daily experiences change me in a profound way. My heart is being gradually transformed. I abide within the ceaseless creativity and transformation of Your Spirit working through me.

Amen

THE THIRD MOVEMENT

The Third Movement helps deepen our awareness of God, the Holy One within the reality of suffering. Suffering is part of life. It just is. It could transform us. It could destroy us. For most people human suffering is something we live with but have difficulty making sense of.

During this movement of the Spiritual Exercises, we will be with Jesus in his suffering. At the same time, we strive to become aware of our personal and unique sufferings, however small or big. As we accept our suffering as part and parcel of life, we ask for the grace of compassion for ourselves and for others and for all of God's creation that is experiencing any degree of suffering.

Suffering is an inevitable reality of living and loving. The older we become, the more we grow in awareness of the reality of suffering and the necessity for compassionate loving.

The Paschal Mystery becomes the blueprint for suffering as we walk with Jesus through the Dark Night of Good Friday and come to the transformation of the Easter morning. The birth, life, death, and resurrection of Jesus are different movements of the same symphony, showing God's extraordinary transformative love for each one of us.

The word "evil" is mostly seen in philosophy and theology books. Spiritual Masters across the traditions use the word frequently while Hebrew and Christian Scriptures both use the word many times over. It is the word also used by poets and artists, but one that is shunned by the hardcore sciences as well as the social sciences.

We do not trust philosophy. We do not trust theology. After all, these are the opinions of people with whom we agree or disagree.

Similarly, we are mistrustful of poets and artists, who just "emote" subjective experiences.

We trust the sciences and the results of research, in which there is neither a concept of evil nor a concept of suffering. That is why we have professional ethics committees who decide what research can or cannot be conducted within our universities and our hospitals. Every university has one of those committees that governs the work of the scientific research. In the sciences, only events and data exist. We analyze them and make statistical conclusions and probability statements and appropriate recommendations.

Our concerns are shaped by science, skepticism, and rationalism. Our critical thinking has kept us from trusting anything or anyone. Suffering and Good Friday do not make sense from the scientific point of view. Redemption, forgiveness, mercy are foreign concepts to the hard-core scientists.

Jesus did not move upward in his position as a prophet. The upward mobility of advancing and succeeding in life has been turned upside down in the life and suffering of Jesus. It appears that evil has conquered good when we experience suffering. End of story. Really? In fact, it is the beginning and a continuation of something very new, only discoverable on Easter Morning. The transformation... The Resurrection...

During this third movement in the Spiritual Exercises, we cannot escape the power of evil in the sufferings of Jesus, in all of humanity or our own sufferings. We cannot help but be affected by the sufferings of all of God's creation, including animals. The one who healed many, comforted and fed thousands, the one who stood for justice and showed solidarity with the poor, the one who affirmed the dignity of every human person, who healed the blind and raised the dead was the innocent life brought before the Roman justice system and handed over to be crucified. The mockery of the Roman justice system. The triumph of evil at its worst.

Evil continues its triumphs today, walking in our cities in the broken bodies of homeless, in the people afflicted with drug addictions and mental illness, in evil behaviors of human trafficking, genocide, wars, abuse of all kinds...

Evil can be overwhelming because it is sinister and deceitful. When it gets into a human heart, it does not have mercy or kindness; it destroys, kills, and tortures. It is dark and terrifying. It underpays fair wages to the workers. It does not share wealth and resources. It does not want any solidarity with the less fortunate. It wants only its own interests.

"But we had hoped he was the one to redeem Israel" (Luke 24:21). One short summary sentence conveys the end of their hope. Yet, the hope that the disciples had placed in Jesus was not momentary but was at the heart of their ongoing lives. And that hope crashed to a halt with Jesus' death on the cross. There is an eerie feeling on Calvary; three empty crosses marred with human blood and stench stand. Everyone is gone, chased away by their fears. Suffering and evil have won.

When it was over, Joseph of Arimathea sought permission to remove the broken, dead body of Jesus from the cross. The women lovingly washed his body, preparing it for the burial and placing it in a tomb that was hewn in a rock. They rolled a big stone to close the entrance into the tomb and left with everyone else, also frightened for their own lives.

The early Christian community read the text that we are reading during Holy Week of the liturgical year of the church, about 100 years after the horrible events in Jerusalem. They were reading and remembering the crucifixion with the resurrection faith, and so we must do the same during this third movement of the Spiritual Exercises.

It is the gift of our resurrection faith that allows us to practice solidarity with all who suffer, regardless of place, societal privilege, or resources that they have. We draw our response directly from our understanding of who Jesus was and what our faith in Him involves. We find in Jesus not a rationalization of why things are as they are, but rather an unflinching confidence that things need not be this way and that unjust structures, such as poverty, hunger, and violence can and will change. We see in the cross of Jesus an assurance that not even death and defeat can prevent the coming of God's Reign of justice and love for all peoples of God. This is the true resurrection. God's Reign is alive in our midst regardless of affiliations, creeds, or social status.

The cross, this symbol of all salvation, is usually placed at the entrance into the sanctuary during the Good Friday services. People come as moved to venerate the wood of the cross. As we do that, each one of us, as an individual and as a community of believers, affirms the sober Christian truth: **we are redeemed sinners, fragile human beings with broken hearts, but with hearts willing to follow Jesus and be the salt of the earth and the light that shines in darkness.** "You are the salt of the earth, but if salt has lost its taste, how shall its saltiness be restored? It is no longer good for anything except to be thrown out and trampled under people's feet" (Matt 5:13). "You are the light of the world. A city set on a hill cannot be hidden" (Matt 5:14).

Some of us might be moved to kiss the rugged wood of the cross to express our gratitude and our sorrow as our hearts embrace Jesus crucified. Some of us might sing quietly that ancient song, "O sacred head, sore wounded, defiled and put to scorn..." (Hymnal #168). Or others may pray, "We adore You, O Christ, and we bless You, because by Your Holy Cross You have redeemed the world." Yet others may perceive the profound truth of the cross that it is an act and an offering of solidarity from God, the Holy One. We in turn must offer that kind of solidarity to one another.

Rowan Williams, the 104th Archbishop of Canterbury, speaking at the Benedictine Spirituality gathering said: "When we fall on our knees before the hard wood of the cross, we are led to recognize the strength and resilience of our selfishness, and the need to let God dissolve the fantasies with which we protect ourselves." (The Episcopal Order of the Holy Cross Newsletter, 2013)

Human suffering culminates in the cruelty of Good Friday. It is God's solidarity with us so that we can live compassionate lives in solidarity with one another, becoming caring and kind people of the One, the Holy One. In this kind of solidarity with God and with one another, evil has very little chance of survival. Suffering can be transformed. The hope of Easter Sunday and the transformation of our hearts becomes the next step on our personal journey to gradual awakenings in our personal life of discipleship.

Seedlings

In the shadow of death

May we not look back to the past,

But seek in utter darkness the dawn of God.

Pierre Teilhard De Chardin, S.J.

•

The Archbishop Justin Welby was giving the inaugural Lambeth Lecture addressing key issues for the Church. He said the following:

> "First, the church exists to worship God in Jesus Christ.
>
> Second, the Church exists to make new disciples for Jesus Christ. Everything else is decoration. Some of it may be very necessary, useful, or wonderful decoration—but it's decoration.
>
> The best decision anyone can ever make, at any point in life, in any circumstances, whoever we are, wherever we are, whatever we are, is to become a disciple of Jesus Christ. There is no better decision for a human being in this life, any human being.
>
> The best decision anyone can ever make is to be a follower of Jesus Christ."

Archbishop Justin Welby, Lambeth Palace, 5 March 2015.

•

Scripture:

Mark 14:12-72	The Lord's Supper
Mark 15:1-47	Jesus Arrested
2Corinthians 4:7-18	Treasures in Jars of Clay

Question:	How do I plan to live my life knowing that there is suffering and there is death?
Practice:	During this time, I will extend my Ignatian prayer time to thirty minutes.
Ritual:	Walking the Stations of the Cross. You can walk the existing Stations at Trinity Cathedral, if you desire.
Grace:	Compassion and Loving Kindness

Prayerful Reflection ...

Jesus my Lord, we keep arresting You and crucifying You. We continue arresting You and crucifying You each time we abuse each other or the natural resources we share. You keep dying and we are indifferent. The destructive forces within us refuse to give up. Instead, we intellectualize them away when we ignore the evidence of death and dying in us and around us.

The poverty and brutal disregard for the dignity of every human being regardless of color and shape of our bodies make us aware that Your suffering continues. It continues in the neglect of our children, in domestic violence, in substance abuse, and refusal to affirm our LGBT brothers and sisters.

Your crucifixion was brutal, but the brutality continues, and we are the ones who are continuing it. We are continuing the brutality in the name of our beliefs and our affiliations. We continue being trapped by comparing and wanting to be better than someone else.

We need Your Holy Breath to transform us to build your Reign on this beautiful island home, the Earth, which You have given to us to care for.

There are so many of us who see this brutality continuing in the suffering of Your people and with misuse of natural resources around us. We kill the prophets who remind us that there is a better way of living this life. We sometimes fall prey to despair.

O, Holy and Loving One, as we stand under Your cross in hope of personal transformations, we ask You to empower us and give us strength to become awakened for the mission of Your justice and Your mercy with love and kindness for all Your creation.

Amen

THREE TYPES OF PERSONS

The First Type: "A lot of talk, but no action" (SE #153).

The first type of person, Ignatius proposes, keeps saying: "I would like to stop being so dependent on all the things which I possess, and which seem to get in the way of my giving my life unreservedly to God."

This type of person has all kinds of good intentions, but always remains so busy about all the "things" that fill up life that death finds such a one still getting ready to make a bigger place for God in life.

The Second Type: "To do everything, but the one thing necessary" (SE #154).

The second type of person, Ignatius proposes says the following: "I certainly would like to be free of all attachments which get in my way of relating to God. I think maybe if I just work harder or I say more prayers or give more money to charity, that would do it."

The Third Type: "To do God's will is my desire" (SE #155).

This type of person Ignatius envisions as someone who says: "I would like to be rid of any disordered attachment which gets in the way of God's invitation to a more abundant life. I am not sure what God is asking of me, but I want to be at a point of balance so that I can easily move in the direction of God's call. My whole effort is to be sensitive to the movements of God's grace in my life and to be ready and willing to follow God's lead."

This person makes efforts neither to want to retain possessions nor to want to give them away unless the service and praise of God our Lord is the motivation for action. Thus, the graced desire to be better able to serve God becomes clearly the motivating factor for accepting or letting go of anything.

Beset by Weakness

The variety of sufferings that we experience in us and around us is enormous – wars, poverty, exploitations, physical and mental illness, intellectual deficiencies, and human trafficking to name just a few. The suffering that each one of us experiences at the core of our existence, however, can be surmised in one word: weakness. "I am not able to find a job because I do not have the right qualifications. I am not smart enough to pass the required exams. I flunked them several times. I have been diagnosed with cancer. I have been diagnosed with mental illness. I hear psychotic voices.

I am depressed. I suffer with autism. I have to apply for Social Security Disability income."

Michael J. Buckley, S.J., as Rector of the Jesuit Community at the Jesuit School of Theology in Berkeley, Santa Clara University, in the spring of 1970, gave a talk to a class of newly ordained priests and invited them to consider the importance of weakness in their new priestly ministry:

> *"As Christians, you and I call ourselves Followers of Jesus. There is nothing more important for anyone than to be called the follower of Jesus, regardless of our weaknesses or our talents. Are you and I weak enough to be followers of Jesus?"*

Fr. Buckley you do not mean weak enough? This must be a mistake. Don't you mean strong enough? No, Fr. Buckley categorically states:

> *"Are you and I deficient enough so that, try as we may, we are unable to ward off significant suffering from our lives? Are we deficient enough so that we live with a certain amount of failure, so that we feel what it is to be an average human being? It is in this deficiency, in this interior lack, in this weakness, in which the efficacy of being a follower of Jesus lies."*

Fleming, D. (2008). *What Is Ignatian Spirituality?* Chicago: Loyola Press.

Using the words written in the letter to Hebrews, emphasizing one's ability to sympathize, Michael J. Buckley continues:

> *"For because He Himself has suffered and been tempted, He is able to help those who are tempted... For we do not have a high priest who is unable to sympathize with our weakness, but one who in every respect has been tempted as we, but without sinning... He can deal gently with the ignorant and wayward, since He himself is beset with weakness" (Hebrews 4:14-15, 5:1-10).*

For most of us, it is easy to forget this profound truth from the letter of Hebrews and live secularized life void of true meaning of being followers of Jesus. Michael J. Buckley emphasizes:

> *"For a follower of Jesus, it is terribly important to enter seriously this revelation given to us in the Letter to Hebrews, of this concurrence between our weakness and being the follower of Jesus... We must dwell upon deficiency as part of our vocation as followers of Jesus. Otherwise, we can secularize our lives into an amalgam of desires and talents, and we can feel our weakness as a threat to our own vocation that was intimated in our baptism. We can easily start doubting that we were never genuinely called to follow Jesus, that we lack the resources that we need to follow him – what we once thought was our destiny and which spoke to our generosity and fidelity."*

Michael J. Buckley, S.J. concludes his homily:

> *"So, it is with us who call ourselves the followers of Jesus—liable to suffering, weak as human beings because we become like him, a gift to others, a kind*

of Eucharist; i.e., an offering of ourselves to the world. We become the Body of Christ.

It is the very liability of the weakness of Christ to suffering that gives us the ability to be broken and shed, that makes the Eucharist possible and our following him more real. How paradoxical this is: The strength of our following Jesus lies precisely in and through the weakness of our humanity."

Excerpts form a homily given to a Jesuit Ordination Class by Michael J. Buckley, S.J., Berkley, CA 1970, http://www.servant-leaderassociates.com/Servant, Leader_Associates/Faith_Perspectives_files/The_Wisdom_of_Rev_Michael_J_Buckley.pdf

MAKING "GOOD ENOUGH" CHOICES

1. **First time for deciding:** SE#175

This is **a time of clarity** which comes with undeviating awareness. We think of the dramatic story of Paul the Apostle on the road to Damascus. This is a time when we feel unmistakably focused in its drawing power.

2. **Second time for deciding:** SE#176

This is **a time when we experience alternating certainties and doubts**, of exhilarating strength and debilitating weakness, of consolation and desolation. We can gain much light and understanding from the experience of consolation and desolation, joy and sadness which are a language of God spoken within our very being.

3. **Third time for deciding:** SE#177

Sometimes, through no fault of our own, nothing seems to be going on. We feel flat or placid, having neither the peace of God's consolation nor the desolation of feeling God's absence. It is at this time that we can still think quite clearly and since we can distinguish no movement from God, we would describe **this time as one of our own deliberating processes.**

•

We appreciate Ignatian guidance in making "good enough" choices. His sensitivity to interior dynamics and the way the Holy One deals with each one of us has stood the test of time. Many have followed his advice and found it helpful.

We could supplement Ignatian insights with a paradigm of behavior change, and making choices that is well researched over the last fifty years. James O. Prochaska,[14] John C. Norcross, and Carlo C. Diclemente identified the stages of change:

Precontemplation: Resisting Change,

Contemplation: Change on the Horizon,

Preparation: Getting Ready,

Action: Time to Move,

Maintenance: Staying There, and

Termination: Exiting the Cycle of Change.

Precontemplation indicates in many situations an active resistance to change and making meaningful choices. The irony is that most precontemplators are doomed to

---

Prochaska, J., Norcross, J., Diclemente, C. (1994). Changing for Good. New York: Harper Collins Publishers

remain trapped in this stage without help from others. The question often arises whether help is even a possibility. During this stage, we do what we have always done, and we get what we have always gotten. We feel demoralized and we consider our past failures.

Contemplators want to change and make meaningful choices. This desire exists simultaneously with an unwitting resistance. The resistance is understandable, since any meaningful action brings with it a terrifying fear of failure. However, awareness is developed during the contemplation stage. We become aware of our defenses and resistances. The process of self-reevaluation, or taking stock, an emotional and cognitive appraisal of our issues and our self can be helpful. This process could reveal to us our essential values and our need for alignment with them.

Preparation takes us from decisions we made during this stage to the specific steps we will take in order to resolve either our issues or create a new direction to our life.

Action to be effective begins with commitment. Once the commitment to change is made, it is time to move; the focus is on the importance of relationships. Awareness of the pitfalls will greatly increase our chance of making "good enough" steps to "good enough choices."

Maintenance takes all that required work and builds on it. Difficult as it is, we realize that negative habits essentially become our friends, and psychologists claim that they become our lovers. They play important roles in our lives. Frequently, they prevent us from making "good enough choices."

Recycling means relapsing. We realize that change we intended to make costs more than we budgeted. We did not budget for complications. Few relapses are intentional. Few people have learned healthy ways of coping with intense feelings. Knowing what to do is essential.

Termination means that we are ready to exit the cycle of change. However, among the experts there is little consensus as for true termination. As for making a lasting choice, there are at least four defining criteria. One, we assume a new self-image that supports healthier behaviors and we begin to own the change that has been elected. Two, we look, think, feel, and act not with false bravado but with genuine confidence. Three, a new lifestyle is essential for successfully maintaining our "good enough choices." Four, finding real solutions means that we can live with our "good enough choices" in ways that reduce the recurrence of self-defeating behaviors.

What we have learned from psychology research with a paradigm of behavior change is very important for spiritual life. Namely, the choices we make have a dynamic process. This means that no one decides anything for ever. We move from precontemplation of a choice into contemplation of a choice. Particularly in the contemplation stage, we get more serious about what is important and what we value. We start thinking of possible action(s) that would move us into the direction of desired choice. Even at this point, we still work on assessing and working through resistances. Only with the help of friends, supportive community of faith and a prudent Spiritual Companion do we finally settle the issues and live out a "good enough choice."

THE FOURTH MOVEMENT

The Forth Movement of the Spiritual Exercises invites us to encounter the risen Jesus after being scared and frightened by the events of the preceding days.

We walk in peace and confident hope as the followers of Jesus. His risen presence is our comfort.

All the Gospels recall that on the second morning after Jesus was laid in the tomb, Mary Magdalene and other women were the first to arrive at the tomb to care for Jesus' body, but his body was not in the tomb.

The story of the missing body and Mary Magdalene's experience as well as the other women of the risen Jesus would be a strange account to concoct. In the Middle Eastern societies of the time, women were not regarded as reliable witnesses; a woman's testimony in court was heavily discounted. And, on top of this, Mary Magdalene was declared by the society of her time as being demon possessed (Lk 8:2). She would hardly add credibility to any story attributed to her. Why then attribute such testimony to women unless that was what was remembered as the truth?

The account of Mary Magdalene as the first witness of the empty tomb was born of a powerful, consistent oral tradition among the earliest followers of Jesus. This is not the oral tradition of rote memorization, the sort that memorizes parables, prayers, teachings and laws, which was also part of first-century Judaism. This is autobiographical memory, a personal experience of the risen Jesus in which stories of these personal experiences are passed on, often colored by the emotional interpretation of those who experienced the events, which shapes the details recalled in the passing on of the accounts. All of those present remember and recount that Mary Magdalene was there first.

In John's Gospel, Mary Magdalene reports the empty tomb to Peter and the other disciple. The two of them run to the tomb; The other disciple also went in, the one who had arrived at the tomb first, and **he saw and believed.** For they did not yet understand the Scripture that he had to rise from the dead.

The initial confusion of the empty tomb: The other disciple known as the beloved disciple, "saw and believed," while Peter and Mary Magdalene "did not understand the Scripture that he had to rise from the dead."

The beloved disciple alone initially recognized the spiritual meaning of the empty tomb.

His understanding will soon be the foundation of the whole church, spurred by the later encounters with the risen Lord. The resurrection of Jesus became the central message of the new community of the followers of Jesus.

When Mary Magdalene and the other disciple encountered the empty tomb, it became the first piece of evidence that "God raised him on the third day and allowed him to appear to all who believe and are the resurrection witnesses."

Later, these witnesses would eat and drink with him "after he rose from the dead."

Only one last task remained: to bear witness that the empty tomb, the end of Jesus' story, was just the beginning.

Seedlings

> "The theory of redemption is a narrative of hope, of 'the Word becoming flesh' to endure suffering and eventually to triumph over death itself through the resurrection. Jesus' life of healing, reconciliation, and teaching is a sign of how the Son is always present, working for the good in our human situations. His death and resurrection reveal how the eternal faithful God will make all well in the fullness of time."

Bishop Dan Edwards
The 10th Bishop of the Episcopal Diocese of Nevada
God of Our Silent Tears

•

Years ago an old municipal lamplighter, engaged in putting out the street lights one by one, was met by a reporter who asked him if he ever grew weary of his work. The old lamplighter said:

> "Never am I cheerless, for there is always a light ahead of me to lead me on."
>
> "But what do you have to cheer you when you have put out the last light?" asked the news writer. "Then comes the dawn," said the lamplighter."

What if we ask the same question of Jesus? One light after another did he put out; the lamp of popular acclaim, the lamp of patriotic approval, the lamp of ecclesiastical conformity all for the sake of God's love, which burned in his heart and showed him the way. At last even the light of his life was to flicker out on the hill of Calvary. What then? We hear the voice: "Into your hands, I commend my spirit." And then came the dawn.

The Lord is risen! He is risen indeed! Alleluia, Alleluia!

Scripture:

John 20: 1-10	The Resurrection of Jesus
John 20:11-18	Jesus Appears to Mary Magdalene
Matthew 28:1-10	The Resurrection of Jesus

Question: Do I choose to be a joyful follower of Christ?

Practice:	Engaging behaviors that cultivate Joy.
Ritual:	Using the Daily Examen to increase awareness of Joyful practices.
Grace:	Praying for the grace of a Joyful heart.

•

Prayerful Reflection...

They crucified You. The nightmare is over. Your body is laid into a tomb. The eerie silence permeates every street corner in Jerusalem. There is no one on the streets, only a dog or two scavenging for food. Everyone is in hiding and talking about the events of the day: the brutal crucifixion of an innocent man, the earthquake, and the tearing of the temple's curtain.

We feel frightened ourselves. We hear Your preaching and teaching on the hills of Galilee. We recall the blind man seeing and the lame man walking. Dear Lord, we feel confused. Now some women went to the tomb and are saying that His body was not in the tomb. They are saying that He showed himself to Mary Magdalene and other women. This is getting too much to be true.

Our fears subside. The eyes of our faith are gradually opening. There is a very cautious joyfulness in our heart—maybe it is true. What do we know! We plan to go to Galilee because He said to our friends to go there and He will meet us there.

This is a hard one to believe. I know you have gone through all these sufferings to show solidarity with each one of us. We understand that we are suffering creatures. We know that you have shown us values of kindness to all Your created beings to alleviate some of this suffering. You challenge us to let go of condemnation of people who live in ignorance and refuse to step into the journey of transformations. We finally got it. Forgiveness, sharing, and solidarity with anyone who is oppressed by poverty and unjust wages, political oppression and lack of resources must be transformed by the message You taught us. There is no room for extreme capitalism or extreme socialism in our societies anymore. There is no room for plundering of the earth's resources to the detriment of our climate. We must learn to live simpler lives and care for each other. We have decided to follow You and become a part of the change that will finally establish Your reign of justice, mercy and love in our midst. You are risen, indeed!

Amen, Alleluia!

Castle, A. (1998) *Quips, Quotes and Anecdotes*. Mystic Publications: Company.

Edwards, D. (2013). *God of Our Silent Tears: Where does suffering come from? What kind of God would permit innocent suffering? What good is God when we suffer?* Los Angeles: Cathedral Center Press. p. 166

CONSIDERATION AREAS FOR SPIRITUAL COMPANIONS

Before you start the sharing time, become mindful of the loving presence of God.

Ask for the grace to see. "Lord, help me to see. I am blind. I want to see." Whatever disturbance you might be experiencing, become aware of it before you engage the following:

1. I name one disturbance that I am experiencing in this moment.

   Requires honesty to acknowledge the objective situation.

   Requires openness to see the difference between my view of what is happening and the actual facts of the situation.

2. I see this situation as "My Path Right Now."

   This is my opportunity to awaken and to see.

It is essential that I understand that my distressful situation is exactly what I need to work with in order to be free, to gain the necessary spiritual freedom to choose My Path in life.

The person I find most irritating becomes a mirror, reflecting back to me exactly where I am stuck and blind.

The irritation is what I add to my being stuck. My irritation and other negative feelings support my blindness.

3. I recognize my most believed thoughts that support my disturbance.

   The deep-seated beliefs often dictate how I feel and act, and they continue to run almost unconsciously.

   The distorted beliefs need to be examined and brought to conversation.

4. What is this that I am experiencing?

   The answers to my disturbances come from entering directly into the immediate, physical experience of the present moment.

   Focus on the "whatness" and not on the "whyness" of the experience.

   The answer comes from being open to experiencing the truth of the present moment as guided by the Breath of God.

Breathe into your heart the truth that you sense. Physically connect with the center of your being. Experience the meaning of this moment.

Extend loving kindness to yourself even when there appears to be no loving kindness in sight.

Sooth yourself with the presence of God.

5. Tell this experience, let it just be for now, for this moment.

   Let your experience be just as it is and rest in God's loving embrace.

   Do not push away your pain. It will not kill you.

Allow the quality of mercy and loving kindness to come because you no longer condemn yourself or your experience. Instead, you simply surrender to God in faith to guide your choices.

When you experience "let it just be," you experience life within the spaciousness of the heart rather than through the self-limiting condemnations of the mind.

Close it with simple prayer: Father, heal me! Jesus, embrace me! The Breath of God soften my heart to the service to others!

Amen!

REPETITION IN PRAYER

Repetition is the return to a previous period of prayer for allowing the movements of God to deepen within the heart. Through repetitions we fine-tune our sensitivities to God and to how God speaks in our prayer and in our life circumstances. The prayer of repetition teaches us to understand who we are in light of how God sees us and who God is revealing Oneself to be for us.

Repetition is a way of honoring God's word to us in the earlier prayer period. It is recalling and pondering an earlier conversation with one we love. It is as if we say to God, "Tell me that again, what I heard you saying?" In this follow-up conversation or repetition, we open ourselves to a healing presence that often transforms whatever sadness and confusion we may have been experiencing the first time we prayed.

In repetitions not only does the consolation (joy, warmth, peace) deepen, but the desolation (pain, sadness, confusion) frequently moves to a new level of understanding and acceptance within God's plan for us.

To use this method, we select a period of prayer to repeat in which we have experienced a significant movement of joy, sadness, or confusion. We might also select a period in which nothing seemed to happen—perhaps because of our lack of readiness at the time. Sometimes, we need a more honest look at our relationships: whether people, a special person, or our relationship with material possessions.

To begin, recall the feelings of the first period of prayer. Use as a point of entry the scene, word, or feeling that was previously most significant. Allow the Spirit to direct the inner movements of our heart during this time of prayer.

If disturbing feelings continue, there might be a need to consult with our Spiritual Companion or Spiritual Director.

PRAYER TIME TO ATTAIN SPIRITUAL FREEDOM

Read contemplatively:

The Rich Young Person from Mark 10:17-31

Follow Ignatian Steps for Prayer:

Place yourself into the loving **Presence** of God.

Attend to your **Desires**.

Apply all your **Senses** and visualize the story of the Rich Young Person

Conversation with Jesus about specific "possessions" that "imprison" or "constantly aggravate me" or keep me "unhappy."

Action: Resolve to engage one behavior that creates inner freedom and joy.

Close: Glory be to the Father and to the Son and to the Holy Spirit.

Spiritual Companion time:

When meeting with your Spiritual Companion next time, share the received graces given during this prayer time. Converse about any actions that you might have decided to take. Any considered action must be tested and given time to mature.

WHAT DOES IGNATIUS MEAN BY POSSESSIONS?

Ignatius wants us to experience God's generosity and God's outpouring of Oneself in creation, especially in creating the human kind, male and female God created us. "So, God created humankind in his image... male and female he created them" (Genesis 1:27). Ignatius suggests that being created in the image of God, we are called to cultivate the inner gift of "Spiritual Freedom." To be spiritually free, Ignatius suggests, is living in a deep relationship with the Holy One from whom we came, in whom we live, and in to whom we will return. For Ignatius having possessions means all our relationships must be subsumed into our relationship with God.

We are fearful to surrender our relationships entirely to the Holy One. We do not want to surrender because we want to keep control of our relationships. To control means to be in charge, to be able to do as we please. To be spiritually free means to cultivate the inner disposition and discern what makes us most alive and content, namely to be our authentic selves.

It could also mean that we lack and are fearful of trusting God. We do not want God to rob us of our possessions because that is all we know and have, and we believe that surrendering our possessions to the Holy One would deprive us of our sense of security. In other words, we make ourselves to be a god of our relationships, namely people, things we own, money, intellectual properties, investments, etc. For Ignatius, all possessions we have are a means to reverence and serve God and in such a way contribute to the realization of God's Reign in our midst. He reminds us that we are not God. We are a beloved creation and expression of the Holy One's love in this world.

•

Accept, O Lord, and treat as your own

my liberty, my understanding,

my memory – all my decisions and

my freedom to choose.

Keep giving me your holy love,

Hold on me your life – giving gaze,

And I neither need not want anything else.

Joseph Tetlow, SJ

THE FIFTH MOVEMENT

The Fifth Movement prepares us for the outpouring of the Breath of Jesus, the Holy Spirit. During this movement, we sense our limitations and open ourselves to receiving the anointing for the ministry of action for daily living, serving ourselves and one another and the world as the followers of Jesus.

We surrender completely to the Lord of Lords, finding the Breath of Christ in everything and in all things. Our intentionality has shifted by now and we sense that our willingness to be working **for the Greater Glory of God** and not for ourselves alone or our particular group is stronger.

The personal striving for inner freedom in everything we do becomes the inner gauge for our motivations.

We are reminded to renew the Baptismal Covenant (BCP pp.304-309) at this time. We are invited to examine the process of our personal conversions with Jesus.

In order to accomplish Spiritual Freedom, Donald L. Gelpi,[15] S.J., Ph.D. in his book *Encountering Jesus Christ* describes the forms and the dynamics of conversion and presents us with helpful guidelines. He states that, in every conversion, one turns from irresponsible to responsible behaviors in some realm of our human experience. For Gelpi, responsibility means accountability **to oneself, to others, and ultimately to God.**

For our purpose, undergoing the Spiritual Exercises, I would suggest that using the word *transformation* instead of *conversion* might be more appealing to the participants.

What does it mean to be responsible to oneself? It means to acknowledge and interiorize values, realities, and ideals that make claims upon us. We stop living in the room of mirrors, living out someone else's expectations, or the expectations of personal impulses and drives, including our cultural expectations. We open ourselves to examine honestly what we believe that matters. Therefore, being responsible to ourselves means to become responsible not only for present choices we make but also for the authenticity of our subsequent choices in some realm of personal experience.

Bergan, J.S. and Schwan, M. (2011) *Love: A guide for Prayer*. Chicago: Loyola Press

Gelpi, D.L. (2009). *Encountering Jesus Christ: Rethinking Christological Faith and Commitment*. Milwaukee: Marquette University Pres

What does it mean to be responsible to others? Not one of us undergoes any kind of meaningful transformation in a vacuum. We are always in relationship with others,

in community. Our motives and the consequences of our choices make a difference to others; hence, we stand accountable to others for both.

The communal aspect of our lives is an essential dynamic in the graced developmental process of becoming, as Apostle Paul would say, the *Body of Christ*, in the world.

As followers of Jesus, we become aware that our personal choices and activities have a ripple effect for the whole community. Case in point, the catastrophic disparity between the rich and the poor. Brutal and extreme capitalistic behaviors do not have room in an authentically transformed life of an individual follower of Jesus. If we were blessed with resources, we also must share the resources we have with those who do not have them. We are responsible also to work on creating the structures that reflect the values of the followers of Jesus. To be a follower of Jesus means to share of what one has with those who are unfortunate and in need of necessities.

What does it mean to be responsible to God, to the Holy One? Our religious transformation is a response to self-revelations and self-communications of God. Each one of us experiences these self-revelations and self-communications of God, the Holy One, in a profoundly personal and unique way. Frequently it is difficult to articulate them in words. These experiences have a claim on us and touch our yearnings to encounter God personally. This is described in the words of Martin Buber who did not like to discuss ideas about God. He was interested in discussing relationships with God, and coined the term *I-Thou* relationship instead of I-It relationship with the Holy One. These experiences may be filled with a sense of ultimate meaning and awe, calling us always to accountable behaviors. In fact, we could say that if religious experience does not call us to accountable behaviors, it may be questionable if not delusional.

We must remind ourselves that we always stand in relationship with God, the Holy One who desires life for us. To have life in us means to be continuously in the process of transformations. This God desires to gradually transform us into the bearers of hope and agents of life in spite of the ashes of our personal destructive behaviors or devastating structures that dehumanize lives.

Transformations vary by focusing on different realms of human experience and by invoking different norms in measuring the authenticity of human behavior.

In **affective transformation,** we decide to begin taking responsibility for the health of our emotional and imaginative lives.

In **intellectual transformation,** we resolve to take responsibility for the truth or falsity of our beliefs, for the adequacy of the frame of reference within which we form our beliefs, and for the validity or invalidity of our thought processes.

In **moral or ethical transformation,** we undertake personal responsibility for the justice or injustice of our interpersonal dealings.

In **socio-political transformation,** we endeavor to become responsible for the justice or injustice of social institutions, including different church institutions.

In the **Christian transformation** process, we take responsibility for our response to the eschatological and normative revelation of God in Jesus and in the mission of His Breath, the Holy Spirit. The Jesus of history becomes the normative revelation of God to us, the Christ of our personal lives.

For us as followers of Jesus, the bestowing of the Breath of Christ makes God a reality of our faith now and in the future.

For the followers of Jesus, Christian transformation begins in repentance, in facing the negative feelings of shame, guilt, fear and anger that prevent or make difficult the commitment of faith.

The healing of repressed negative emotions through repentance yields an enhanced esthetic sensitivity to religious excellence. This is the degree of truth and goodness in any reality. It is the excellence embodied in Jesus and in the people whose lives resemble His motives and who desire to follow Him. As Paul advises, we must put on the mind of Christ (Colossians 3:9-17) and practice behaviors worthy of our baptismal covenant.

The transformations described above are always in process. They are not linear. They have their own dynamics commensurate with our abilities and our willingness to follow Jesus the Christ. The ongoing Christian transformation transvalues the other conversions by suffusing them with Gospel values and with the charismatic empowerment of the Breath of Christ, the Holy Spirit. The ongoing personal Christian transformation allows the Breath of

Christ to sanctify us and to continue making us into the Holy People of God for the service of all God's people and of all God's creation.

And so, we imagine ourselves as members of a community of believers, the Body of Christ, living out our Baptismal Covenant for the greater Glory of God the Father and the Son and the Holy Spirit.

We continue reminding ourselves, as Ignatius Loyola prompts us, that love must always manifest itself more in deeds than in words alone.

Seedlings

Love consists in sharing

what one has

and what one is

with those one loves.

Love ought to show itself in deeds

more than in words.

Ignatius Loyola, S.J.

Mighty God, Father of all,

Compassionate God, Mother of all,

Bless every person I have met, ...

bless every city, town, and

street that I have known,

bless every sight I have seen, ...

Great God bless the world.

John J. Morris, S.J.

Eternal Father, confirm me;

Eternal Son, confirm me;

Holy Spirit, confirm me;

My one and only God, confirm me.

Ignatius Loyola, S.J.

Glory be to God for dappled things—

For skies of couple-color as a brinded cow;

For rose-moles all in stipple upon trout that swim;

Fresh-fire-coal chestnut-falls; finches' wings;

Landscape plotted and pierced—
fold, fallow, and plough;

And all trades, their gear and tackle and trim...

With swift, slow; sweet, sour; a-dazzle, dim;

He fathers-forth whose beauty is
past change; Praise him.

Gerard Manley Hopkins, S.J.

Scripture:

Acts 2:1-21	The Coming of the Holy Spirit
John 15:26-27, 16:4-15	The Work of the Spirit
John 14:8-17, 25-27	Jesus the Way to the Father

Question: How do I structure my life since I have encountered Christ Jesus?

Practice: Daily Prayer time of Thirty Minutes focusing on the Breath of God, the Holy Spirit, encompassing me, empowering me, awakening me.

Ritual: Spiritual Companionship on weekly basis.

Grace: Come Holy Spirit, the Breath of Christ, and kindle within me the fire of your zeal!

Prayerful Reflection...

In your presence, dear God, You whom I call the Holy One, I find myself at the end of my Ignatian Spiritual Exercises retreat. I know you have created me, and you continue creating me. I am grateful for the gift of life you have given me. I sense the grateful heart within me.

In this journey of gradual awakenings in Christ Jesus my Lord, I have encountered You in a very personal way. You are the Lord of my childhood and my teenage years. You have been present in my life at every step of all my transitions from childhood to my mature years and now in my growing old years. I have not always realized Your gentle and sometimes slow-moving activity of Your love and care at every juncture of my living.

Despite my limitations and fragility, I have stepped forward and You have anointed me in Baptism and have claimed me as Your own forever. Only in encountering You, dear Lord Jesus, do I realize that I experience you, the loving and embracing parent.

Now I feel vulnerable and tender. You have broken my heart open. I beg that Your Holy Breath imprints into my awareness of my very being the love for myself and the love for Your people. This pilgrim and wondering people can organize themselves and work together in establishing Your reign of justice and mercy for all to enjoy. Give us your grace and Your love. This is enough for each of us, to be the instruments of Your creative care and love.

As for me, I offer myself to You entirely in the service that is in harmony with Your design and Your life-giving purposes.

Amen

CONTEMPLATION TO ATTAIN DIVINE LOVE

First Point SE #234

Ignatius invites us to call to mind the blessings of all creation, the blessings of redeeming works of Jesus the Christ. Ignatius wants us to name the special favors we have personally received.

We pray with gratefulness how much God our Lord has done for us. This generous God has shared with us of God's possessions. Finally, we bring into prayer how much this same Lord desires to give of One own very self to us, of One own divine life.

Then we consider, according to all logic and justice, what we ought to offer to the Holy One, the Divine Majesty, the God Oneself. Thus, moved by great feelings of generosity, we make this personal offering:

> "Take, Lord, and receive all my liberty, my memory, my understanding, and my entire will, all that I have and possess. Thou hast given all to me. To Thee, O Lord, I return it. All is Thine, dispose of it wholly

according to Thy will. Give me Thy love and Thy grace, for this is sufficient for me."

Second Point SE #235

During this second point we pray how this generous God acts in the whole of the universe giving existence, in the plants giving them life, in the animals conferring upon them sensation, in human beings specially giving understanding. We pray how God dwells in each one of us gives us existence, life, sensation, intelligence. We are created in the likeness and image of the Divine, the Holy One.

We pray again as stated in this second point...

Third Point SE #236

Focus your prayer now on how God works and labors in the whole universe and in each one of us, in all creatures upon the face of the earth, that is, God conducts Oneself as one who labors. Thus, in all the cosmos, the elements of the earth, the plants, the fruits, the cattle, God gives existence, conserves them, confers life and sensation.

We pray again as stated in this third point ...

Fourth Point SE #237

During this Forth Point we imagine how all blessings and gifts are coming from the Holy One. Our limited powers come from the supreme and infinite power of God. Justice, goodness, mercy, joy, forgiveness, everything comes from God as the rays of light come from the sun.

We pray again as stated in this forth point ...

•

When ready we conclude The Contemplation to Attain Divine Love with one of our favorite conversations. You might ask as to what the favorite conversation has been during our engagement in the Spiritual Exercises thus far? Was it with Jesus or maybe with Mary, the mother of Jesus, or Peter or someone else like the Holy Breath of God, the Holy Spirit? Choose this person now, speaking exactly as one friend speaks to another in a conversational fashion, back and forth, sharing feelings, thoughts and hopes for now and the future. Conclude this time of prayer with a prayer of your own preference or you may choose the prayer like Our Father...

ONGOING PERSONAL RELATIONSHIP WITH THE HOLY ONE

The Contemplation to Attain the Love of God is the culmination exercise of all the Spiritual Exercises that you have been engaging thus far. Ignatius intended it to be the climax point.

The Pilgrimage to Discipleship, the personal relationship with God within the community of followers of Christ comes to its new beginning. The love of God which is referred to here is not only God's love for us, which is always given, but the focus is now on our love for God, the Holy One. This prayer should take between 30 and 60 minutes.

It is important to remember that for Ignatius, prayer is mainly of the heart, not of the mind. This prayer is not meant to be a process of conceptual reasoning, but of reflection engaging memory, understanding and imagination, leading to a new and deeper appreciation of reality. We see things now as they really are.

Ignatius' detailed directions and points are for guidance only. In this, as in any prayer, do not follow the directions as if they were a recipe, but use them to lead into a deeper interior conversation with God, the Holy One.

Before the actual time assigned to this prayer, Ignatius makes a note to remind us of the true nature of love. ***He wants to warn the person praying against the easy confusion of love with sentimentality. Love is expressed in deeds and in giving. Words and sentiments are inadequate.*** He also reminds us that we know God's love by God's actions and God's Self-giving. We know God's love by experience, not by theory, and this prayer seeks to make us conscious of the experience. It is this sacred experience that deepens our relationship with the Holy One now and forever. John H. Wright, S.J. suggests that true love changes our interiority, thoughts, affectivity and our behaviors. Our thought processes shift. Our affectivity shifts. We express love in deeds and in the service of giving as we pray:

"Looking to the past,

with gratitude;

To the present,

with peace and joy;

To the future,

With trust

And assurance of hope!"

Wright, J.H. (1979). A Theology of Christian Prayer. New York: Pueblo Publishing Company, p.115, and in personal conversations.

CLARIFYING AND OFFERING IN IGNATIAN WAY OF PRAYER

The first step, reminding ourselves of the Holy One's presence, serves to place us in the mood for prayer. Here we picture God in his transcendence, as absolutely other, and ourselves before God as dependent creatures. This image of the transcendent God is the traditional image that most of us grow up with and internalized. When we praise, petition, and give thanks to God in prayer, it is to the God who is outside of and beyond us.

The second step is our desires. We want to be explicit about what we are seeking in prayer. We are often unaware that everything we are and have is a gift. During this step of Ignatian prayer, when paying attention to all our desires, as well as our most authentic desires, we ask for the awareness or "interior knowledge" of the truth of our desires.

The body of Ignatian prayer, consisting of mindful presence of the Holy One, paying attention to personal desires, visualizing a scene, conversing and acting, present to us different aspects of God's immanence. It is God who is joined to and active in all of creation, including ourselves and our activity. This image of the immanent God has often been neglected. God is not only a one-time Creator, but God sustains on a continuing basis, provides and cares for this creation. God is not only a one-time redeemer but is continually redeeming and making all things holy.

Concepts of the immanence and the transcendence of God are only concepts, and God is beyond any concepts we can form. ***In Ignatian prayer, we are not seeking an understanding of the concept of God, but an experience of the living God.*** We seek an awareness of the experience of God who is giving, indwelling, laboring, and emanating in ourselves and in all creation. These are some of the aspects of God's immanence that Ignatius asks us to contemplate.

The experience and interior knowledge of love, shown by the dynamics of God as active in the world and in ourselves, leads us to a response of love, which is expressed in an offering of ourselves to God. The Ignatian prayer, "Take, Lord, receive" expresses the totality of this offering. In the completeness of God's self-giving, we experience an equally complete self-offering:

**"Take, Lord, and receive all my liberty,
my memory, my understanding, and my
entire will, all that I have and possess.**

**Thou have given all to me.
To Thee, O Lord, I return it.**

**All is Thine,
dispose of it wholly according to Thy will.**

**Give me Thy love and Thy grace,
for this is sufficient for me."**

Puhl, L. J. (1951). *The Spiritual Exercises of St. Ignatius*. Chicago: Loyola University Press, p. 102

IGNATIAN PRINCIPLES FOR MAKING PRAYERFUL DECISIONS

How do we know what we desire to do with our lives at any given time and at any given stage of our life cycle? This question prompts us to engage Ignatian teachings on "Discernment of Spirits" that are dynamic and practical.

By now we have developed our spiritual muscles and have become convinced that God desires life not only for us but also for others and all creation. To "discern" means to figure out our genuine wants and desires and place them before the Holy One and then listen attentively to the movements of our inner stirrings as revealed in our unique emotional landscape. Ignatius calls this process "Discernment of Spirits." It is not a simple task. Most of us desire to have clarity about our desires. Some of us believe that we know what is good for us and what we want to do with our lives. Ignatius encourages us, therefore, to take discerning time and become familiar with our personal emotional landscape and our genuine and authentic desires commensurate with our abilities.

Ignatius Loyola did not invent the "Discernment of Spirits." He builds on a long tradition of discerning "God's will" that goes back to the Hebrew Scriptures, continues through the Christian Scriptures, and is further developed by the various schools of spirituality within Christianity, such as the Benedictine, Franciscan, Anglican, Lutheran, Dominican, Episcopalian, Presbyterian and Methodist traditions, to name just a few.

Building on the Christian spiritual traditions, as a master observer of the interior movements of the spiritual life both in himself and others, Ignatius articulated helpful guidelines for the discernment that have stood the test of time over the past four and a half centuries.

A key moment leading up to his Christian conversion, or as we called it earlier transformation, occurred when he was defending a castle against a French invasion and his leg was hit by a cannonball. While convalescing from the resetting of his shattered leg, which he asked to be re-broken and reset so he would look better in his courtly tights, he asked for some romance novels to read. However, the only two books available for him to read were a Life of the Saints and a Life of Christ.

He spent part of his time lying in bed daydreaming about future courtly adventures and serving some unidentified lady of his dreams. When he daydreamed about these chivalrous adventures, he felt excited but afterwards felt flat, empty, and mildly depressed. When he dreamt about serving God as Benedict, Francis, Dominic, and the other saintly followers of Jesus whom he was reading about, he felt peace and contentment. He felt consoled, happy and joyful, rather than depressed, as he did after his courtly daydreams. He noticed this difference and concluded over time that God was calling him, not to continue as a courtier, but to do great things in the service of God, as did the saints he read about.

Ignatius continued to reflect on the different "spirits" or "interior movements" he experienced. Eventually he included this knowledge in his retreat manual called *The Spiritual Exercises.*[16]

Ignatius assumed in his discernment of spirits that God communicates directly with each of us in our "hearts, minds, and souls" through various interior movements as experienced in our feelings, thoughts, and desires. However, Ignatius was not so naive as to think that all our thoughts, feelings, and desires were caused by the Spirit of the Holy One. Some indeed are holy desires that come from God, while others come from other sources like "negative spirits," ultimately from what he called "The Enemy of our Human Nature." So, to figure out which of our inner desires, thoughts, and feelings are from God, and which are not, is the goal of "discernment of spirits" proper. To help us with this, Ignatius developed his rules or guidelines for the "discernment of spirits." Today, however, when we apply Ignatian insights about discernment, we must also be aware of developmental and neuropsychological sciences and the contributions they have made. The importance of medications that many of us take and how they interact with interior movements of the Spirit must be discussed with your spiritual companion and incorporated into one's discernment process. We either educate ourselves

---

Fleming, D. (2013). *Draw Me Into Your Friendship: The Spiritual Exercises, A Literal Translation and a Contemporary Reading.* [5, 16, 24-26, 149-55, 169], Numbers refer to the paragraph numbers of the Ignatian text. All quotations from *The Spiritual Exercises* are taken from Fleming's contemporary reading of the *Spiritual Exercises.*

by research or consult with trained professionals when engaging the process of discernment of spirits today. Stable mental health, substance use abstinence and as well as relative physical health are the prerequisites to engage successfully Ignatian "Discernment of Spirits".

Before introducing someone to Ignatius's insights on discernment, let us consider the following:

First, "discernment of spirits" always involves choosing between two life-giving values such as between two good things and not between good and evil. If our decision is between something good and something evil, that's not a matter for discernment. We need to do what we know is right or what is just, kind, and loving.

Second, "discernment of spirits" only makes sense in the context of a personal love relationship with God, the Holy One. Ignatius says that love expresses itself more in deeds than in words. If we love someone, we want to please that person. If we love God and want to have a relationship with God and grow closer to God, we will want to please God, serve God, and do "God's will." It's only in this context of a love relationship with God that the question of how we know God's will or let us call it "God's dream for us," becomes meaningful. It is a belief of this writer that God works within our authentic desires. It is within our authentic desires that God's dream for us becomes most palpable as well as most evident.

Third, "discernment of spirits" comes out of the spiritual warfare images and the cosmology of Ignatian time and struggles described by the desert fathers and mothers and in the Bible, itself. If there were no inner struggles, if "God's will" for us was perfectly clear, there would be no need for the "discernment of spirits." However, we all struggle with our false self, inner compulsions, selfishness, pride, anger, greed, fears, self-doubt, lack of trust, and being co-opted by the values of our surrounding culture. In Biblical terms, the cosmic struggle between good and evil is being played out on the stage of our hearts. We must take sides. Who and what are we for and against?

Guidelines

Keep in mind that the genuine and most authentic desires of our heart reside in the place where the Holy One and we meet, in prayer.

Also keep in mind that the dream which the Holy One has for us is built upon our unique personality and our unique abilities as well as cultural opportunities in which we find ourselves. We remember here the words of Thomas Aquinas who said that grace always builds on nature, which means on the unique qualities that make us who we are. The new research in the field of neurosciences is helpful here and must be incorporated in the process of discernment. Seeing the larger picture about discernment and grace, the words of Thomas Aquinas are crucial because he was referring to the fact that all of creation is a theatre of grace, the stage upon which the drama of our salvation unfolds.

Authentic Discernment Process

At the beginning of the *Spiritual Exercises*, Ignatius spells out basic attitudes or qualities that a person must have as preconditions for entering an authentic discernment process of seeking "God's will." They are the following:

Openness*:* We must approach the decision in question with an open mind and an open heart. We cannot find "God's will" for us if we enter into the decision-making process with a pre-conceived outcome based on our biases, and what Ignatius calls "attachments," that is, an attitude of "I already have my mind made up, so don't confuse me with the facts!" "Attachments" refer to areas in our lives where we limit freedom and put conditions on a decision. An example could be:" I'll go to college anywhere ***if*** it's within a day's drive of my parents' home."

Generosity*:* To enter into a decision-making process with such openness requires a generous spirit with which we, with a largeness of heart, put no conditions on what God might call us to. Some spiritual writers use a metaphor. This is like writing God a signed "blank check" and letting God fill in the amount and content of the check. Only a generous person would do this.

Courage*:* Such openness and generosity require courage. God might be asking something authentic of us, challenging, and risky. It takes courage to give up control and trustingly put the direction of "my little life" in God's hands. There's no telling where God might be calling us, but gradually it becomes clear and more focused and authentic. To be that open and generous takes courage.

Interior freedom*:* To make such a prayerful, generous, courageous decision requires interior freedom. Ignatius describes three types of people and their differing approaches to decision-making, SE #149-155:

> The **first type** is "all talk and no action." This kind of person is full of good intentions, but remains so distracted by his or her busyness about so many relatively inconsequential things that they never get around to the "one thing necessary," namely, "God's will for them," God's dream for each one of us personally. Not to decide ends up being their decision.
>
> I have experienced people "discerning" a possible vocation in life, a possible state of life or possible lifestyle: "Should I become an engineer, a physician or a teacher? Should I go to graduate school or just get a job, get married or divorce, have a family or consider an ordained ministry in my church like diaconate or priesthood, or should I leave the ordained ministry of my church? Should I consider joining a different church to accomplish what is authentic with who I am?"
>
> Discerning how to live with personal sexual orientation must become a subject for "discernment of spirits." Integrated sexuality most often involves authentic behaviors based on the Gospel values spelled out in the Baptismal Covenant (BCP pp 304-305). Not acting becomes reactive. Living reactively erodes authenticity and a sense of integrity of the Baptismal Covenant.

The **second type** of person does everything but the one thing necessary. These people may do all kinds of good things in their lives *but* don't face the central issue of what God is calling them to do with their lives. They are, in effect, putting conditions on what God can call them to. They'll do good things as long as it doesn't ask too much of them, especially demanding a total commitment that would call them to adjust their priorities to what God is asking of them and thus put "God's will" first in their lives. An example could be, "I'll enter into any career as long as it will support me in an upper middleclass lifestyle." This would preclude a lot of options God might be calling us to!

The **third type** of person is the only one who is truly free. Their whole and genuine desire is to do whatever "God's will" is authentically for them with no conditions attached. This is the attitude necessary to find and follow God's authentic dream for us. Ignatius calls this personal posture spiritual freedom.

Having One's Priorities in Order

There is a logic to Ignatius's spirituality. If serving God, our Creator and Lord, is the ultimate goal of our lives, then everything else in our lives must be kept in the subordinate position of a means to that end. This means that things such as opportunities, experiences, and relationships are to be valued and chosen only insofar as they contribute to our ultimate goal in life and rejected insofar as they deter us from that goal. "What we want above all is the ability to respond freely to God, and all other loves for people, places, and things are held in proper perspective by the light and strength of God's grace."

In coming to a decision, only one thing is important: to seek and to find how God is calling each one of us at this time and moment. God has created us out of love. Our salvation is found in our loving God and the returning of that love. All our choices, then, must be consistent with this given direction (*SE* #16, 169, 23). For example, states of life such as marriage or divorce, single life, life in a religious community of men or women, or ordained ministries in the church like being a priest or deacon are *means* to serving God. We also serve God in our chosen career like employment and the kind of work we do. In other words, everything we choose to do with our lives, we must put in perspective of serving God first. Keep in mind that any of these discernment endeavors are always being done in a community of believers which assist us to discern our suitability for a specific election that is being considered. We never discern personal life choices leading to an "election," as Ignatius advises, on our own. A spiritual director or companion or a larger group of supporting friends frequently proves to be helpful.

Not Confusing Ends with Means

Ignatius comments, "it becomes obvious how easy it is for me to forget such a simple truth as the end and goal of my whole existence when I consider the manner in which choices are often made." Many of us, for example, choose marriage, which is a means. We then only secondarily consider the service and praise of God our Lord in marriage. Many of us first choose a lucrative employment to make a lot of money or to be successful, and only afterwards we choose to serve God by it.

All of these people exhibit an attitude of putting God into second place, and they want God to come into their lives only after accommodating their own wishes and dreams. In other words, they mix up the order of an end and a means to that end. What they need to seek first and above all else, they often put last (SE#169).

One of the examples of confusing ends with means, mentioned above, is a person who first chooses a lucrative career and is to be successful and only afterwards looks at how they might serve God by making charitable donations or volunteering. A person like this, in effect, puts God into second place, only wanting God to come into their lives after first choosing what ***they wish***. They mix up the order of an "end" and a "means to that end," not putting first things first.

Having these essential attitudes of openness, generosity, interior freedom, prayerful reflection on experience, having one's priorities straight, and not confusing ends with means, the discerner has their satellite dish pointed in the right direction in order to receive God's signals. Possessing these qualities is the precondition for hearing God's invitation through an authentic discernment process.

Practical Discernment Points

1. Ignatius suggests that we start the decision-making process by putting before ourselves what it is we want to decide. For example, we might be trying to decide whether to divorce or stay married,

move into an ordained ministry of the church, apply for a new job, or enter a new relationship.

2. He then asks us to pray for the grace to "be like a balance at equilibrium, without leaning to either side" (SE # 179). In other words, we should strive to the extent possible not to prefer one option to the other, but only desire to do "God's will." To help us maintain focus and perspective, he asks us to keep the ultimate end and goal of our existence clearly before us.

3. Then we pray for God to enlighten and move us to seek only what is most conducive to God's service and praise.

4. Ignatius suggests, using decision we are considering, to imagine a person we never met, who seeks our help in how to respond to God's discerning movement. We then observe what advice we give this person and follow it ourselves. This is helpful, since most of us are better at giving others advice than at figuring out what we should do.

5. Another suggestion is that we imagine ourselves at the end of our lives either on our deathbed or after our death standing before Christ. How would we feel about our decision then? What would we say to Christ about the decision we have just made? We should choose now the course of action that would give us happiness and joy in looking back on it in hindsight.

6. When we do not experience inner clarity about the correct decision to be made, Ignatius

suggests that we use meaningful reasoning to weigh the matter carefully to attempt to come to a decision in line with our living out God's will in our lives. Bearing in mind our ultimate goal, to do this we should list and weigh the advantages and disadvantages for us of the decision at hand, for example, the reasons for and against one decision or the other. We are then to consider which alternatives seem more reasonable and filled with meaning and decide according to the weightier motives. Looking over our list of "pros" and "cons" for the decision at hand, we should notice if any of the reasons listed stand out from the others, and why, and see which way this might point us. This technique can help us move from inner confusion to greater clarity, at least as to the issues that need to be attended to and help separate out which are more significant.

7. Having come to a decision and made the election, we turn again to the Holy One, to God and beg for signs of God's confirmation that the decision is leading us toward God's service and praise. The usual sign of this confirmation from God is an experience of peacefulness about the decision. The confirmed decision has a feeling of "rightness" about it, and we feel a sense of God's presence, blessing, and love. This is a very important step, since the feeling of rightness, peace, and joy about a decision is a positive indicator that we have made the right decision and the right election, whereas

feelings of anxiety, heaviness, sadness, and darkness often indicate the opposite.

Summary Points

Look at the decision prayerfully from many different points. Take time making the decision, be patient, trust the process, and ultimately trust that the Holy One, the Lord of all will lead us to the right place, when we do our part to the best of our abilities.

Follow what our heart and gut tell us to do and what seems right and meaningful to us. In life decisions and matters of the heart, we rarely feel complete certainty and clarity. This is more than a rational process. However, once we have considered the decision prayerfully, consulted others we trust, and have attained all the data we reasonably can, we take a leap of faith and make a choice and an election.

"Discernment of spirits" takes us on an exciting adventure of trusting God. When we give up control and take risks to follow God's lead not knowing where we will end up, with the attitudes of openness, generosity, and inner freedom recommended by Ignatius, life is a lot more fun and exciting than when we try to control everything ourselves.

We need to trust that God is not going to lead us off a cliff! It is important that we remember that God is a loving God who wants us to be content and is going to lead us to a good place where we will find joy, fulfillment, and contentment.

That doesn't mean that where God leads us will not involve sacrifice and even some suffering. We remind ourselves that sacrifice and suffering is a part of living. But it will lead to a life that matters, makes a difference, has great meaning, and involves more joy than we could ever imagine. Contrast this to a life where we try to control everything and only follow our own self-determined plans.

Any life worth living involves discernment. Prayerful discernment will most probably lead us into making choices, and making choices always includes saying goodbye to some other possibilities that are equally attractive. But, if we are following God's call, whether that be a state of life or vocational pursuit, marriage or divorce, single life or a life in a religious community of men or women, a life of a physician, a nurse, a psychologist, a teacher, a firefighter, social worker and many more, the "good enough" discernment usually brings satisfaction, contentment and joy.

Dyckman, K., Garvin, M., Liebert, E. (2001). *The Spiritual Exercises Reclaimed: Uncovering Liberating Possibilities for Women*. Paulist Press: New York

Seedlings

In the Gospel of Luke 17:11-19, Jesus tells the ten lepers to go and show themselves to the priests. As they were going, they were cleansed. Only one who was a foreigner returned to give thanks to God for the gift of healing. Then Jesus said to him, "Stand up and go; your faith has saved you."

Stand up and go. Stand on your own two feet, but be faithful to the God, the Holy One who walks with you every step of the way as you discern your life's directions.

Stand up and go. Be honest with yourself and with others as you listen to the heartbeat of the Holy One's embrace in your life. Work the best you can. In all things and for all things, be grateful and follow the promptings of the Spirit, of the Holy Breath of God, guiding you and showing you the way.

Let generosity flow from your gratefulness. Teach others that the Holy One lives in our midst and desires life for us. And all these things teach your children, if you are blessed with having them. They will thank you one day.

But most of all remember that we must be willing to let go of the life we planned, so as to have the life that is waiting for us. Ignatian Discernment of Spirits is one way to find the way.

Writing a Statement of Personal Christian Identity

There are several components of our personal identity that we must consider. First, there are a number of theories that address development components of personal identity. The paper authored by Justine Poll and Timothy Smith (Journal of Psychology and Theology, 2003, Vol. 31, No2, 129-142) leads to understanding the richness of development of the personal identity as well as personal spiritual identity.

Second, what we want to accomplish during the Spiritual Exercises, the practice of regular prayer, is to write a clear statement to ourselves and to our personal community of believers about our Christian Identity.

The components of this statement include the following:

- My covenantal promises at baptism (BCP, pp 304-309).

- My recognition of the process of personal conversion (affective, intellectual, moral/ ethical and socio-political and, in particular, personal Christian conversion)

- Awareness of the stages of spiritual identity development that have been researched and are helpfully spelled out in the paper mentioned previously.

    1. **Pre-awareness** of the self as an eternal being in relation to God. At this point, individuals do not consciously regard themselves in spiritual terms.

2. **Awakening** of awareness of the self in relationship to God. Individuals at this stage begin to recognize events or interactions in spiritual terms.

3. **Recognition** and recollection of other spiritual experiences, such that the initial awareness obtained in the previous stage is progressively generalized to an awareness of spiritual experiences in other settings and interactions.

4. **Integration** of spiritual experiences with self-concept. Spiritual experiences typically seen in previous stages as external to the person become internalized, simultaneous with the development of spiritual relationships, person to person, and person to God. Individuals recognize at this stage their own spiritual nature, and they perceive and interact with the world accordingly. They spontaneously take in and seek out spiritual experiences because doing so has become for them a way of life.

A STATEMENT OF PERSONAL CHRISTIAN IDENTITY

I am aware that I am being created lovingly and that I was knitted in my mother's womb by the loving God. I believe that God is the one who creates, sustains, redeems, and sanctifies me.

I am choosing to be in a covenant relationship with God. I decide daily to follow Jesus as my Master and my Lord. I call myself to be a follower of Jesus in a Christian Church, the Episcopal Church in the United States of America, which embodies the system that allows for transformation, respecting the dignity of every human being.

For me to live is to love. I believe that I am suffused with God's presence and am charged with it. Where there is love, a consistent sense of God's presence happens.

As Ignatius teaches me, I come to believe that God works within me and labors for me in all creatures upon the face of the Earth. For me, God is the Laborer even in the midst of most difficult suffering situations. The world consists of God's activities converging around me, giving me glimpses of hope.

All the blessings and gifts that I experience come from above as the rays of light descend from the sun. God is the source of loving because God is love within Oneself.

I work on accepting myself totally. Just as God accepts me, I am practicing acceptance of myself. I choose to see my own beauty and my own power against the backdrop of God's "loving-ness."

May this God who creates me, sustains me, and sanctifies me give me grace to be a person of action to spread the Good News of the Reign of God in our midst.

Glory be to the Father and to the Son and to the Holy Spirit...

FOR ONGOING CHRISTIAN PILGRIMAGE

Completing the Ignatian Spiritual Exercises retreat is an experience of a unique spiritual awakening. The question we ask now is, "What am I awakened to? I have been blessed with many spiritual experiences during this retreat. I have gained several insights. They are refreshing my very inner being. But what am I awakened to?"

We are awakened to the reality of understanding that our brokenness is real. Our self-absorbed behaviors could be malignant and that continuing to behave in the direction of our self-interest only does not produce life, neither for me nor for anyone else. We are realizing that behaviors from self-interests only are in contradiction to our Baptismal Covenant.

We repent and ask for God's forgiveness and God's grace to assist us in organizing our lives with simplicity and generosity of sharing. We have come to believe in common good for all of God's creation. We are aware of the interconnectedness of all creation. This awareness prompts us to advocate for justice and dignity of all human beings and of all creation. We are relational beings wherever we may be. Our personal ways of doing things affect everything around us.

Ignatius introduced us to the meditation on Two Standards earlier in the Spiritual Exercises. One standard is the standard of Christ and his values and the other standard is the standard of darkness and the systemic evils and its values. It confronts us to continue applying the values of the Gospels and spelled out in the Baptismal Covenant. We made the initial commitment in our Baptism. We have renewed the Baptismal commitment to follow the standard of Christ during this retreat. We continue applying the Baptismal values in our daily living to the best of my abilities and God's grace. We are developing a clearer sense of being a disciple.

We spent a great deal of the Spiritual Exercises prayer time following Jesus on his travels from Bethlehem and Nazareth, to the sea of Galilee and to Capernaum. Our inner beings are set on fire with desire to follow Jesus more dearly, intimately and closely. He is our Lord and our God. We have been invited to relate to God as Abba, Father. We have been invited to live a life of solidarity with all those who suffer in any way because of injustice, poverty, or greed. We are being introduced to the ways of mercy and generous sharing of whatever possessions we have material, intellectual, affective, and spiritual.

The sufferings of all God's creation must become the area of concern to us. We are all suffering creatures. Suffering is a part of living. It just is. It must be alleviated, and any unnecessary suffering must be removed. We dedicate our lives to assisting and guiding human beings to remove the sufferings they can and create a life of human dignity – be that individually or institutionally.

Immersing ourselves into the suffering of Jesus, the way of the cross, we understand better what solidarity entails – walking with, supporting, and joining all those who suffer unnecessarily because of systemic evil – be that in the corporations of the world or the organizations that continue discrimination, racism of any kind, and victimization of the innocent. However, just as the early Christian Communities remembered the suffering of Jesus with the Resurrection Faith, so do we choose to participate in solidarity with all those who suffer with personal resurrection faith and the community of believers with whom we share that faith. For us the Resurrection Faith means that evil of any kind will not have the last word. It is the transformations in Christ, present and future, that have the last word.

In the Acts of the Apostles, we have learned about the outpouring of the Holy Spirit, the Holy Breath of life, upon the followers of Jesus. That same Breath of God has empowered us for the mission of God's Reign amid God's People. "May Your kingdom come! May Your will be done on earth as it is in heaven."

Now I come to the very core of the Ignatian Spiritual Exercises: The Contemplation to Attain Love. This Ignatian Contemplation dispels many doubts in us.

In the Principles and Foundation, we have discovered that there is a purpose to our "little life." This purpose is accomplished by practicing spiritual freedom that facilitates unique service and mission. We are called to gratitude. We respond in mutual love between You and us, Lord, and between us and Your People.

We are aware that we are accepted and affirmed by You, Lord. It is Your love for us that welcomes our response of freedom and gratitude which overflows into love of our neighbor.

Dear Lord, we are being invited to continue discovering Your creative life in all things, in the ordinary and extraordinary. What this means is radical commitment to this world – to everything and everyone in it. We choose to engage in responsible actions to protect the natural resources of the earth. We choose to do all in our power to love, as You would love, generously. We realize that loving as You would love includes placing each one of us in solidarity with all Your People throughout the world. Give us Your love and Your grace to accomplish this.

A helpful companion at the completion of the Ignatian Spiritual Exercises is the *book* of a friend, theologian and counselor Thomas Hart,[17]entitled *Coming Down The Mountain* published by the Paulist Press. I recommend this insightful daily reader for a single purpose, that of integrating the Ignatian Spiritual Exercises you have just competed to your daily life. It might provide you with a language that you need in order to articulate your own experiences with a freshness of a competent Spiritual Guide and writer.

Another suggestion at the close of your retreat is a compilation of fifteen meditations written by Jacqueline Bergan[18]and Marie Schwan, CSJ. It will become a sure

---

Hart, T. (1988). *Coming Down The Mountain: How to turn your retreat into everyday living.* Paulist Press, Mahwah, New Jersey

Bergan, J. and Schwan, M. (1991). Praying with Ignatius Loyola. Loyola Press: Chicago

companion on your journey of ongoing discipleship inspired by the spirituality of Ignatius Loyola.

Remember, at the heart of Ignatian Spiritual Exercises is to allow ourselves to be transformed by the Holy Breath of the Holy One to become, gradually and authentically, instruments of the Reign of God in our midst. Once we experience this transformation, Ignatius encourages us "to go forth and set the word on fire" with God's love, compassion and mercy.

Go Forth
And Set
The World
On Fire
with mercy
and
loving kindness!

Ignatius of Loyola

TESTIMONIALS

In his book published 2014, *Inside the Jesuits, page 35,* Robert Blair Kaiser makes a testimonial to his personal experience of the Spiritual Exercises of Ignatius Loyola:

> "On the thirtieth and final day of the retreat, I dedicated myself to this Arsonist of the heart. To sum up, I acquired a new way of looking at the world and my place in it. The world I saw had been redeemed by God-becoming-flesh and charged with God's grandeur. It was a world in which I could see God in all things and all things in God, a world that I could love and enjoy and help make a better place – if I cared to be a "saving" presence in my own time and place."

•

People make the Spiritual Exercises for a variety of reasons. Many want to find clarity about their life direction. Others desire to deepen their discipleship with Jesus. For Andrew Garfield when he asked to undergo the experience of the Spiritual Exercises, there was a need to prepare to play the lead role in Mr. Scorsese's new film, "Silence." This is what he says about the experience in an interview published in The Jesuit Review of Faith and Culture, *America, January 23, 2017:*

> "The main thing that I wanted to heal, that I brought to Jesus, that I brought to the Exercises, was this feeling of not-enough-ness. This feeling of that forever longing for the perfect expression of this thing that is inside each of us. That wound of not-enough-ness. That wound of feeling like what I have to offer is never enough.
>
> This is my sincere prayer. I'm praying that I'm freer to offer myself vulnerably..."

•

> "I am forever grateful for the opportunity to participate in the Spiritual Exercises of St Ignatius. My experience may have been somewhat unusual in that I have gone through the practices with a group three separate times.
>
> You might have thought that after the second-year experience, I would be ready to sail alone. Not so; I wanted more. And after the third year, I can truly say the exercises are now part of my whole being. Each day of my life is a journey with my Lord and best friend, Jesus. How I react to my inner voice, how I encounter others, and most of all how I encounter my God, has greatly changed me and enriched my life."
>
> Joyce

•

"During the first meeting, I ran out as I didn't want to share my feelings and myself with others. But I came back, partnered with another participant, and soon learned to trust and participate more fully. The most memorable moment during the Spiritual Exercises was when we were asked to visualize the scriptural passage of Jesus in the Garden with two of His disciples. He was praying but the disciples fell asleep. I could tell Jesus was distressed so I went up to Him and placed my hand on His shoulder. He seemed comforted. It was a very defining moment for me. Through these Ignatian Spiritual Exercises, I have learned to quietly listen and to pray in a special way."

AH

•

"The first gift I received was my Spiritual Companion, my prayer partner. Our weekly meetings were a sacred space.

The second aspect was my time in prayer using the Ignatian Way. One experience stands out when I was praying the post resurrection account of Jesus and Peter in John 21. I had been struggling to decide whether I belong back in my previous life vocation. Placing myself in the scene, I heard Jesus tell me, 'Don't get back in the boat. Follow me.'

In His Name now, I am moving on with deeper faith and hope."

Michael

•

"I learned that I was part of God's creation and all my needs mattered to God. I can feel God's presence.

I have been able to put order in my prayer life. This affirms the trust I have in God and His Presence in my life.

Some amazing changes came about, such as one person making a change in vocation.

Although I realize that much work is needed to know God's plan to serve Him, I feel that I have grown spiritually having completed the Spiritual Exercises and I am more sure of God's loving plan for me."

Ruth

•

"I experienced the power of the Spiritual Exercises of St. Ignatius in 2015 and have since followed the format several times a week. The Exercises have transformed my way of praying and have helped me focus on how I conduct myself each day as I strive to become a more devoted follower of Jesus. What I especially enjoy is (1) the conversation phase where I both speak and listen to Jesus or to someone in the Gospel passage, and (2) the action phase where I make an intentional commitment to carry out that same day. "

Rene

•

"Those weeks in the Spiritual Exercises were transforming and gave me further insight into my spiritual self. It was a time of deep inner reflection and self-examination that were sometimes painful. Throughout the process, I kept asking God what the path is you have set for me. I became comfortable to ask the question: "What is my desire?" The answer came towards the end of the Spiritual Exercises. It came in bits and pieces, but when we were asked to think about what our mission as followers of Jesus is, it all pointed towards the vocation of being a permanent diaconate in our church.

Patsy

•

"I have taken the Spiritual Exercises twice with each time being different and so rewarding in ways I never expected. My love for my Lord and Savior continues to grow and when I stop and listen – truly listen – I feel a surge of love that nearly overwhelms me. Such pure love!

I intend to engage the Ignatian Spiritual Exercises again and am sure it will be quite different than either time before. As I change and deepen my following the Lord, the spiritual exercises change right along with me."

Lindsay

APPENDIX A

PRACTICE OF SPIRITUAL DIRECTION

Nature of relationship:	Spiritual Direction relationship is *fiduciary*, like a professional relationship. Confidentiality is a sacred obligation knowing also its limitations. The holder of the confidentiality privilege is your directee.
Frequency of meetings:	During the duration of the Spiritual Exercises, it might be necessary to meet one time every week. After the Spiritual Exercises Experience, one time a month. It is important that the directee, however,

	takes responsibility for the rhythm and frequency of meetings.
Length of meetings:	Sixty minutes with clear understanding of the importance of time boundaries, beginning and ending of meetings.
Place of meetings:	Preferably professional office or other suitable place like church or parish offices. Avoid meeting with your directee in your home. Become mindful of the violation of emotional and space boundaries.
Fees:	Most spiritual directors charge a sliding fee of fifty or one hundred dollars. It is important to have a clear financial arrangement with your directee prior to beginning of spiritual direction, preferably in writing, one including when the fees are collected. When the spiritual director assumes responsibility of engaging in the practice of spiritual direction as a part of his/her salary agreement with the parish or with the Rector or the Vestry, the

financial arrangements also need to be made clear.

Requirements: Spending daily time in prayer of no less than 15 minutes.

Points of clarifications Between a Spiritual Director and a directee:

1. Agreeing on the goals or outcomes of spiritual direction.

2. Understanding and learning about the unique history and the salvation story of faith of the directee.

3. Working with the levels of present experiences in prayer; learning the language of prayer experience; assisting the directee to pay attention to the unique quality of the relationship with Christ, the icon to God and his or her inner landscape of faith.

4. Becoming aware and sharing with your directee the particular dynamics of how he/she interacts with God and how God interacts with your directee. Observe and articulate the connections

between prayer experience and the way the directee engages life of the Gospel values.

Closures:	To begin and to end the agreed time shared in spiritual direction is necessary. It is an essential part of the spiritual direction process. The beginnings and endings are part of life and there is a need to honor that. Close with a short prayer.

APPENDIX B

BENEFITS OF REGULAR SPIRITUAL COMPANIONSHIP AND SPIRITUAL DIRECTION

1. Awareness of singleness of **purpose.** The helpful question to keep in mind: Why am I here or why am I doing this spiritual direction or companionship?

2. Awareness of Christ as the "**Way**", (Jn. 14:6). The question to keep in mind at this point is Who am I? Am I a follower of Jesus? Am I still ambivalent?

3. Awareness of inner workings of God's Breath in my daily life and in my **prayer practice.** What do I really want?

Presence of God: Invitation to myself and my companion – Lord open my lips, and my mouth. We shall proclaim your praise! "For where two or three are gathered in my name, there am I among them." (Matt 18:20)

Empathy: Pause after each person speaks and consciously relax. While pausing, with acceptance and curiosity ask yourself: What is happening now? What am I feeling now? What might this person be experiencing?

Compassion: Elicit feeling friendly toward yourself. Visualize sending these feelings toward yourself, and toward your companion. Practice loving kindness to all beings in the name of Christ Jesus.

Decreased stress and anxiety: Bring your attention to your experience of breathing. Pay attention to any feelings of anxiety and fear. Notice how they shift from moment to moment. Just allow what is to be there for now. Ask what is my experience right now? Notice the sensation of each in and out breath. Expand your awareness to your whole body with an attitude of acceptance.

4. Experience of Community. We are relational beings. The way we relate to each other we relate to God. "Now you are the body of Christ, and each one of you is a part of it." (1 Corinthians 12:27).

5. Ongoing Practice of Discernment. It presupposes that we are open and engaged in the process of transformation on all levels, including – Intellectual Conversion, Religious

and Spiritual Conversion, Affective Conversion, Moral or Ethical and Socio-Political Conversion. An authentically converted Christian lives in openness to the Breath of God, the Holy Spirit, who anoints each one of us to live authentically as followers of Jesus the Christ.

APPENDIX C

PAYING ATTENTION TO OUR DESIRES

Ignatius Loyola (1491-1556) studied theology and Latin at the University of Alcala and then in Paris. He was schooled in the philosophical thoughts of his time.

He identified the various motives that lead a person to choose one course of action over another. He named the process of choosing "discernment of spirits." The goal of discernment is to choose well. Ignatius calls this choice of choosing well "election."

The central point in the Ignatian discernment and then election is our willingness to pay attention to our authentic desires and align them with the desires that the Holy One has for each one of us living on this beautiful planet Earth, which is a meaningful and abundant life now and forever.

Ignatius recognizes the inherent creative tension in the discernment process of making election(s).

What is a human desire that seems to be so central to Ignatius? Ignatius would most probably assert that human desire is the fundamental motivation of all human action. Desire is a sense of longing or hoping for a person, object, or outcome. It is a tension between an individual and the thing or state that the individual desires, apparent reaching out toward the desired object or person or state.

Our authentic and genuine desires, Ignatius suggests, could be a sacred place where the Holy One and we meet. I express my desires to the Holy One and deepen my desires by thinking about them, by feeling them, by sensing them and discerning how they fit into the context of my life's journey as an intimate follower of the one who has a claim on my life, Jesus the Christ. They are intricately correlated with the stages of my personal developments: physical, social, emotional, moral, spiritual and intellectual.

My desires are intrinsically connected to my needs and my wants and the very person that I am becoming. Ignatius is not talking about my capricious needs and wants. He seems to be concerned about my authentic needs and wants to affirm my selfhood and my genuine sense of well-being that are in relationship with others. We must remember that for Ignatius "discernment of spirits" is always between life giving values or two possible goods that I desire.

My best chance of fulfilling my desires is to develop a relationship with God and communicate my inner desires by converting the inner voices of my desires into my outside voice. I communicate to the Holy One what I inwardly desire by uttering it outwardly. "Jesus my Lord, I desire to accept my past, including my family of origin and ethnicity and my gifts as well and limitations. I desire to focus my energy into the present time of my living. I desire to create a meaningful work now that would support me.

I desire to have an intimate companion in my life. I desire to have resources to travel. I desire my child to be successful enough to live well. I desire to be free from depressions, or excessive anxieties, or my insatiate cravings for new experiences. I desire to become more social and learn to relate to people in a relaxed and engaging way. I desire either living a life of comfortable solitude or I desire more involvement in social justice issues of our time. I desire to make changes towards a better balance."

Each of us has developed an internal filtering process that helps us choose which parts of our constant inner monologues get voiced outside of our heads. Sometimes the choice is based on what we consider to be polite or appropriate, using subtlety instead of directness to try to get our point across. Other times the choice is made based on our expectations of the other person and what we feel they should know about us, our feelings, and our needs or wants. But, our best chance of getting what we desire is to communicate specifically by converting our inner voices to our outside voice, my voice. The voice of my desires. May the daily prayer practice bless this new practice in my spiritual life.

You may say that God knows my desires, so what is the point to state them outwardly? This may seem unnecessary, especially when we think that God has the same information we ourselves are working with at this time and at this moment.

We have to remember that it is helpful and often necessary to communicate precisely. It is necessary to hear our own voice, to hear our own voice of our unspoken desires. Doing this minimizes the chance for misinterpretation. It also makes the voicing of our desires an act of birthing them. We convert our desires present in our thoughts, our feelings, our sensations and our imagination to sound, releasing them from the chamber of our minds into the outside world, into the Holy One's loving embrace. This voicing of our desires carries energy and intentionality with it, making our thoughts, wishes, and our dreams become utterances to the Holy One who "labors for us and with us in everything," as Ignatius Loyola asserts.

When we have the courage to speak our minds and use our voice to send the desires from our inner world to the world outside, we take a bold step in claiming them. By removing fear of what the Holy One may think and removing the expectation of what the Holy One should understand, we free ourselves and our desires from the bondage of keeping them hidden in the mental chambers of our minds. We let loose our desires and project them unto the One who is Love, the Holy One. Remember the healing story from the Gospel of John (5:1-18), where Jesus asks the man who was sick for a long time, "Do you want to get well?" He told Jesus his desire to get well.

Next time we become aware that we have a choice about how to communicate with the Holy One about our desires, we can choose to use our outside voice and watch its creative power at work. We might be surprised to discover that our own desires might be very much in tune with what God desires for each one of us. When we discover the attunement of our desires with the Holy One's desires for us, we might be ready to enter into, what Ignatius calls, "making the election." For example, I desire to reaffirm my commitment in marriage. I make a statement loud and clear of what I desire so that I hear the uttering of my desires. If the attunement is healthy, an inner sense of well-being ensues. If the attunement is not healthy and is forced, an inner disturbance most probably could follow. We always remember, using our contemporary language, making the election means that we choose well for what is most authentically us, but always between two good things. Choosing well for ourselves means affirming others as well, the person or the people of the Holy One. "I want a divorce. I am not able to be authentically myself in our marriage. I have been consulting several professionals. I always come to the same conclusion, which is that divorcing is my only way to create my own authentic self. I feel peace and I choose to remove myself out of this marriage."

As we choose well for ourselves, we give glory to the Holy One. Again, using Ignatian language, Ignatius would say that making good choices is always for "the Greater Glory of God."

> "In every good election, insofar as it depends on us, the eye of our intention ought to be single. I ought to focus only on the purpose for which I have been created, to give glory and praise to the Holy One and to labor with the Holy One in such a way that would make me fully alive and fully human, as we work together, in establishing the Reign of God, now and forever" SE #169-188.

APPENDIX D

PERSONAL LETTER TO GOD

"God is the one who began this work in me,
and I am certain that God won't stop before it is
complete on the day that Christ Jesus returns.
I must keep going in the direction that
I am now headed."

Philippians 1:6, 3:16

Dear God:

I am mindful to be in your presence...

Name and signature:

Date:

"For the greater Glory of God"

Ignatius Loyola

APPENDIX E

IGNATIAN SPIRITUAL EXERCISES IN A NUTSHELL

- The Way (Baptismal Pilgrimage)
- Singleness of Purpose (Discipleship)
- Practice (Prayer)
- Community (Companionship)
- Discernment (Affective, Intellectual, Ethical, Socio-Political and Christian Transformations)
- Action (Decisions, Elections)
- Ongoing Transformation in Christ (The Breath of Christ, the Holy Spirit makes God a reality of our faith now and in the future.)

ABOUT THE AUTHOR

Julius Mataric Rogina, Ph.D. was born in Zagreb, Croatia, December 10, 1945, which at that time was Socialist Federal Republic of Yugoslavia. After attending a Jesuit High School in Zagreb, he elected to enter the Croatian Province of the Society of Jesus on July 31, 1962 and was ordained a priest on June 29, 1975 by Cardinal and Archbishop Franjo Kuharic of the Archdiocese of Zagreb, Croatia.

The Spiritual Exercises of Ignatius Loyola not only attracted him as a young Jesuit scholastic, but the experience provided him with the inner matrix for becoming a committed follower of Jesus.

After sixteen years of Jesuit formation and life in a community of brothers, he elected to leave the Jesuits to marry and raise a family. It was a difficult time to say goodbye to his Jesuit lifestyle and his Jesuit brothers. He always felt at home in Jesuit communities wherever he lived. But a deep desire to marry and have a family was equally powerful. He had to choose between two equally good values. He made the Election.

After a prolonged discernment process, he left the Jesuits and proposed marriage to Patrice Pantarotto. They were married on June 8, 1979 and brought three healthy and beautiful children into the world: Kreshimir Louis, Mira Elizabeth and Teresa Claire. They have taught him what it means to be dad and a loving father.

His marriage to Patrice ended in a divorce. For those who have gone through a divorce after a long marriage, he shares the pain: the questioning wrenches the soul. The practice of Ignatian Spiritual Exercises helped him profoundly in the process of healing after the divorce.

After engaging in "Spiritual Discernment," Julius made another Election in his life and in July of 1986, he found a home in the Episcopal Church, was received as a priest by Bishop Stewart Zabriskie of the Diocese of Nevada, where he was able to practice his unique ordination gifts. V. James Jeffrey, Rector of Trinity Episcopal Church, welcomed him and assisted him in the process of transitioning from being a Latin Rite Roman Catholic priest to becoming a priest in the Episcopal Church, USA, a member of Anglican Communion. Fr. Jeffrey created room for Fr. Julius at Trinity Cathedral where Julius offered the Spiritual Exercises of Ignatius Loyola on an annual basis. The *Pilgrimage to Discipleship* was born out of this context.

Today, Julius continues his profession as a Clinical Psychologist both in private practice and at the Medical School, Department of Psychiatry and Behavioral Sciences, University of Nevada, Reno. As a clinician, he is interested assisting his patients and his students in finding meaningful and purposeful life and living. He believes, as Viktor Frankl, his mentor, frequently taught that, "life is not primarily a quest for pleasure, or a quest for power, but a quest for meaning. When we can't find a deep sense of meaning, we distract ourselves with unhealthy pleasures."

As a priest he continues to assist at Trinity Episcopal Cathedral in Reno, Nevada and a wider Episcopal Diocese of Nevada.

His soul is knitted out of the matter of the Spiritual Exercises of Ignatius Loyola. It is Fr. Julius's desire that the pages of this guide assist you in your pilgrimage to find and follow Jesus with deep faith and affection.

December 10, 2018

Reno, Nevada

AMDG

Frankl, V.E. (1984). Man's Search For Meaning. New York: Touchstone, p. 117

Frankl, V.E. (2000). Man's Search For Ultimate Meaning. Cambridge: Perseus Publishing, p. 140

ABOUT THE BOOK

This book is a guide to the Spiritual Exercises of Ignatius Loyola. It is intended to assist a person on the unique Christian Spiritual Pilgrimage of faith and encounter the God of life. Applying insights of one of the great masters of Christian Spirituality and insights of contemporary psychology, the reader is introduced to the five distinct movements of Christian spiritual living. Topics covered include understanding human brokenness, encountering Jesus of Nazareth and the Christ of Christian worship, coming to grips with human suffering and redemption, living with resurrection hope and accepting the gift of the Holy Breath of God, rules for discernment and election. Playing an active role in finding a spiritual companion and experiencing the benefits of ongoing spiritual direction is discussed. Readers will be challenged anew by the richness of Christian Spiritual Tradition grounded in our baptismal covenant and as viewed through the lenses of Ignatius Loyola.

CPSIA information can be obtained
at www.ICGtesting.com
Printed in the USA
LVHW061137141019
634126LV00018B/5031/P